A tired marriage can be revitalized!

Millions of people do not recognize the source of their conflict and head for divorce in total despair. Others simply tie the knot tighter and hold on begrudgingly for decades with practically no hope.

That's too much to ask — **and it's totally unnecessary!**

Marriage burnout is immensely easier to prevent than it is to cure — **but cure is possible.** With new life pumped into the relationship, scores of happy years can lie ahead.

Keeping Your Marriage from Burning Out

WILLIAM L. COLEMAN

Here's Life Publishers
P.O. Box 1576, San Bernardino, CA 92402

First printing, July 1989

Published by
HERE'S LIFE PUBLISHERS, INC.
P. O. Box 1576
San Bernardino, CA 92402

Library of Congress Cataloging-in-Publication Data
Coleman, William L.
    Keeping your marriage from burning out / William L. Coleman.
      p.   cm.
    ISBN 0-89840-254-9
    1. Marriage—Religious aspects—Christianity.   2. Burn out
(Psychology).   I. Title.
BV835.C597   1989
248.8'4 7dc 19   89-30706
                           CIP

Scripture quotations are from *The Holy Bible: New International Version,* © 1973, 1978, 1984 by the International Bible Society. Published by the Zondervan Bible Publishers, Grand Rapids, Michigan.

For More Information, Write:
L.I.F.E.—P.O. Box A399, Sydney South 2000, Australia
Campus Crusade for Christ of Canada—Box 300, Vancouver, B.C., V6C 2X3, Canada
Campus Crusade for Christ—Pearl Assurance House, 4 Temple Row, Birmingham, B2 5HG, England
Lay Institute for Evangelism—P.O. Box 8786, Auckland 3, New Zealand
Campus Crusade for Christ—P.O. Box 240, Colombo Court Post Office, Singapore 9117
Great Commission Movement of Nigeria—P.O. Box 500, Jos, Plateau State Nigeria, West Africa
Campus Crusade for Christ International—Arrowhead Springs, San Bernardino, CA 92414, U.S.A.

Contents

*T*hanks

No author can thank them all.
Too many people have helped
in classes, in seminars
and even standing on street corners.

A few couples, however, deserve particular notice
for sharing with me. They are:

John and Juanita Regier
Cliff and Jessie Jensen
Larry and Jolene Fox
Howard and Gloria Bartlett
Rich and Lois Janzen
Junior and Jan Nachtigal
Rodger and Deanna Langemeier

I also want to thank the Grace Brethren Church in Norton, Ohio, for giving me feedback on some of this material.

Naturally, I have changed the stories, even the ones from the coffee shop, enough to disguise my friends, counselces and relatives.

*T*urn *U*p the *F*lame

Every once in a while you meet a couple who sparkle. They don't just grin and bear it. They aren't putting on their happy faces. You sense the fact that they enjoy each other and are comfortable in one another's company.

That's the way marriage should work — with a feeling of anticipation, with a dash of excitement, with an aura of hope. Every couple deserves enough fuel to keep the flame burning, both in their brightest moments and when the cold winds rattle the door.

As you read this book, try to keep a few facts in mind. God never intended us to drag through life, snorting, grunting and protesting. Rather, He supplied us with enough energy, enough challenges, enough good times and enough surprises to keep our marriages filled with living.

So throw another log on the fire and listen to that marriage crackle. It's one of God's better gifts.

Bill Coleman
Aurora, Nebraska

Candidates for Marriage Burnout

WHEN MARK AND PEG Were first married, they were cuddlier than a couple of prairie dogs on a chilly night. They touched, hugged, snuggled and kissed every time they got close to each other. A day at the park or revarnishing an old table together were their ideas of fun. As long as they were together life was filled with a special kick.

As time went by, however, they seemed to lose some of their zip. Exciting evenings gradually turned into hours of watching television. As they passed in the hall, neither bothered to reach out and make contact.

Peg said, "Our marriage is all right but it certainly isn't the same as it used to be. Now we seem to move along at a pitiful pace. The flame is still there but it's not about to set the woods on fire."

She speaks for millions of wives whose marriages have entered the maintenance stage. These couples keep going, work their jobs, clean their houses, watch reruns and bump into each other in bed once in a while. There isn't anything wrong with their marriage, but the spark isn't there either. Their relationship simply is. Little else can be said for it.

We really aren't too concerned if our marriage has its ups and downs—the nature of human beings almost demands that—but we should be bothered when the downs start appearing more often than the ups, and they stay longer. When this happens, our once strong, healthy marriage may be entering the first stages of burnout.

Category A—Low Achievers

Peg and Mark fall into category A of marriage burnout, the *lifeless relationship*. Their partnership has fallen to a low survival level, barely receiving enough fuel to keep the flame going. One of their biggest problems is colorless boredom. They go through the motions. If their marriage ever breaks up, it will be for lack of energy rather than from a big explosion.

We frequently imagine marriages dissolving after a long series of heated battles, name-calling and threats. That certainly happens. However, a large number of marriages merely pass without a whimper. No shouts or epithets—they just die from inactivity and boredom. Neither partner committed high crimes or conducted colorful escapades—they simply had no reason to continue.

If you had a dollar for every marriage that folded out of sheer boredom, you could buy a home in the Alps. These couples aren't fighting; they aren't chasing affairs; they aren't looking for new horizons. Tired of looking at the back of the evening newspaper, and fed up with banal conversation at the supper table, they see no point in going on. They find a divorce lawyer because the hearings will provide a bit of excitement. Don't think I'm kidding.

The author of Ecclesiastes sounds ready to give up. He says, "All things are wearisome, more than one can say" (1:8). Discouraged, he doesn't have an ounce of gas left in him. It's the normal experience for a category A relationship, sooner or later.

In our own marriage Pat and I spent many years simply stumbling through the relationship. Each stage seemed new to us. Forced to learn the hard way, we suffered a lot of knots on our heads. Like standing at the curve of a train track, we seldom saw the train until it had roared past us.

We continuously felt overwhelmed. Then three little preschoolers flooded us. Near poverty conditions stunned us. The inability to get a babysitter and the probability that we couldn't pay for one anyway frustrated us. The need to adapt as our personalities grew and changed left us spinning. And naturally my career came first. If I failed every relationship in life, my career had to be crowned a "success."

If we'd had more and better information, we could have done what we do now: stand back and ask what our marriage needs. It's no fun buying a ticket after the train has passed.

This is not to say that we hated our marriage, but sometimes we just lost control, or we ran out of coal. We couldn't chug up another mountain or take another curve. The old gauge would sputter on empty.

Today we have learned to keep watch on our marriage. Rather than let it run us, we have decided to take the controls. Now when we begin heading for the dumps, we stop and discuss the problem. We take time out *before* we reach the curve to share feelings, set goals and find vital spiritual meaning. We can never again allow our marriage to be a derelict train.

Our marriage relationship remains fragile, just like yours, but that frailness reminds us that we must keep the fuel coming to keep the flame alive, just like you do. Loving couples wake up and resuscitate their relationships before they expire.

Category B — High Attainers

Category B of marriage burnout is the high attainers. Their relationship *gets left behind*. They work day and night, own two expensive cars, ski twice a winter and attend night school. Riding in the fast lane, chasing goals at a torrid pace, they need huge quantities of fuel merely to keep up with living. With their relationship tied irreversibly to their external accomplishments, they seldom carry enough fuel to go around, and they burn up what they do have too quickly. If their marriage blows up, the explosion will be spectacular. At the speed they are traveling, there are no quiet accidents.

All of us have met couples who started their marriages with impossible schedules and dreams. One that I remember was Chad and Vicki's. During the first three years of marriage, they jumped in over their heads buying furniture, joining clubs and charging new clothes. They moved to a Chicago suburb, landed fast-moving jobs and swiftly began climbing the mountains of their dreams. After thirty-six months their marriage and their dreams began to fall apart just as rapidly.

Chad and Vicki were highly competitive. Each of them wanted to take the fast elevator to the top of his or her profession. Setting sales records and producing incredible charts were paramount to them, and they both understood where they were coming from. Extra time was spent winning racquetball trophies and heading up fund drives.

"We didn't *flunk* our relationship — we just didn't have time for one," Chad explained. "The outside pressures were so great that we had no energy left to give to each other. We did everything we were supposed to. We even had sex. It was quick and furious — just the way we thought it had to be."

Most of us consider burnout a *job*-related syndrome. However, the same symptoms ruin millions of *marriages*. People — good people, people with outstanding intentions — are switching marriage partners as if they were changing careers. Frequently they are Christians who wouldn't hurt anybody. They launch out, like an unplanned military maneuver, with little thought of how they will supply the operation. Later, they cancel the exercise because they can't sustain it.

Choices We Can Make

Most of us have not reached the brink of destruction,

yet. We still have a pile of wood in the backyard and occasionally stoke a fair fire for an evening. Yet we realize that the woodpile isn't as high as it used to be, and it may not be enough to hold off hard times. We resolve that, before it runs out, we will restoke and revive the blaze. It will be good to see the flames laughing over the logs again.

Fortunately, there are some definite steps we can take to bring that about. Rather than being intricate plots of clever psychological twists designed by mental gymnasts, each is a practical, levelheaded step within the grasp of any caring couple.

When you as an individual suffer from burnout, one of two things must be changed: (1) You must *reduce the need* for fuel; or (2) you must *increase the amount* of fuel.

The same choice must be made in a marriage. If it is burning out, you: (1) *are expecting too much*; or (2) *are not giving* your marriage *enough* fuel to keep the flame alive. One or the other (or both) needs to be adjusted.

Don't let the simplicity of this formula throw you. It's a familiar one. For example, if you can't make your car payment, you either have too much car or too little money. You have to change one of them. Solutions do not have to be complicated to be effective. They just have to be implemented.

There are definite areas where a deficiency can indicate a serious problem of underlying burnout, and where fresh fuel needs to be supplied.

The great thing about this is that if those areas of weakness are identified early enough, they can be reversed.

MARRIAGE BURNOUT IS IMMENSELY EASIER TO PREVENT THAN IT IS TO CURE,

but cure is possible. With new life pumped into the relationship, scores of happy years can lie ahead. Unfortunately, millions of people have not been able to recognize the heart or the source of their conflict and have divorced in total despair. Others simply have tied the knot tighter and held on begrudgingly for decades with practically no fuel. That's too much to ask, and it's totally unnecessary.

Careful couples confront an issue as early as possible and revitalize their love, happiness and commitment. We used to think marriages should just hang together. Today we know better. Long-lasting, pulsating marriages live because the parties involved make conscious efforts to keep their strengths intact.

Growth is essential to normal relationships. If a couple fails to grow, their relationship almost inevitably faces expiration. The failure to develop is devastating and it results in each individual feeling futile. As they feel increasingly useless, they are bound to turn their frustrations onto the relationship.

Burnout in marriage is not isolated and cannot be treated as such. If other areas of our lives are suffering, they will spill over into our partnership. For this reason, in the following chapters we will address a variety of subjects such as jobs, finances, sex, spiritual goals, masks, sacrifice, commitment, romance, expectations, personal fulfillment, and more.

So take courage. We will ask a lot of questions, but we will find a lot of answers, too.

Flexercise

1. Did you identify with any of the couples mentioned in this chapter? Which one? In what way?

2. Is your marriage too exciting? Too boring? Just right? On what do you base your evaluation?

3. What specific problems can you pinpoint in your marriage that may be leading to burnout?

How Is Your Fuel Supply?

HOW DO YOU KNOW if your marriage is burning out? Let's turn the question around. (Being positive is much more uplifting.) How do you know if your marriage is *not* burning out? In all probability several strong points are evident.

Satisfied Couples

To get some clues as to where your marriage stands, answer the following questions — but be honest with yourself; this isn't kid stuff.

1. What four things do you find most satisfying about your relationship?

Name them specifically. Broad, sweeping statements seldom give an accurate picture. A general feeling may mean you are playing games, refusing to face reality.

Are you and your spouse happy to talk to each other? Do you look forward to non-critical conversations such as sitting together for coffee or a sandwich? If you center every conversation on problems, there may not be enough wood in Oregon to keep you going. Bills, repairs, orthodontists and traffic tickets are not the sole topics of great marriages. If each talk is a headache, we soon learn to stop talking.

- If you can still talk after several years of marriage and enjoy it regularly, you must have a substantial supply of fuel. (If you have problems in this area, your conversations can be brought back to life. We will find the ways a little later.)

Do you enjoy going places together—not where you *have* to go but where you *want* to go? If your relationship consists of heading in separate directions, the lack of contact will hurt both. That's also true of going to the same locations separately. How frequently do we do that? We both agree to go, but for all practical purposes we might as well be on either side of Mongolia.

- Satisfied couples like to go as a pair. They can stand being apart, but they prefer being together. (The lack of this desire can be resolved, too.)

Do you look forward to seeing your mate at the end of the day? You used to provide each other with a positive spark. You could hardly wait to share, listen, feel each other's presence in the room. Or has that been replaced with a knot in your stomach or, just as bad, no sensation at all? Do you get the same excitement from observing the newspaper bounce off the porch as you do seeing your partner?

- If his arrival still gives you a tingle, the fire is burning. (If not, it can be rekindled.)

Are you satisfied with your partner's physical love? Age may be a factor in this answer, but only a tad. A recent study in Sweden revealed that 50 percent of the males and 40 percent of the females surveyed were still sexually active at age 70. At age 80, 12 percent of males were still involved. The researchers at Goteborgs Sahlgrenska Hospital are convinced that those who gave up sex experienced a drastic drop in memory and intelligence.

- Happy couples are, generally speaking, happy in bed (Proverbs 5:19). (If you're not, take heart — you can be.)

This is only a beginning list. You can add to it to fit

your own situation, but it dare not be ignored. Couples must find their relationship satisfying. It is unrealistic to nurture a marriage where neither party is excited about being there.

2. *How are you handling change?*

The inability to cope with change is bound to leave a couple anemic. Change is a regular part of life, and it is intensified when two people live together. We change in our temperament, size, interests, dreams, ambitions, moods and other departments. Solid partners expect alterations over the months and years, and they react well to them.

Change is one of the few dependable events in life. We don't know if we are going to be rich, healthy or live to be a hundred. But we do know we will change.

Those who cannot adjust as the changes come will necessarily burn out. It's like a wheel that has locked and refuses to turn. The rest of the vehicle is moving along rapidly but one major part is incapable of functioning. Such rigidness has to cause considerable damage.

When each partner in a couple progresses at a different rate, or they grow in separate directions, they invite friction. In order to manipulate the dangerous curves, the drivers must see change as welcome, refreshing and challenging.

The average couple switches careers several times during their lives. They move from area to area. Normally they alter their hairstyles, clothing and recreation dramatically. Ten years later each finds himself married to a different person though he has remained with the same one.

Randy and Chris are excellent examples of surviving through extensive change. They began their marriage as a one-career family in a quiet area of Detroit. He was happy working in an auto plant, and she enjoyed doing housework and raising their children.

After a few years he became discontent in the factory and took a job in sales. The change meant long hours and unpredictable income. In the meantime, Chris went back to school in search of something more fulfilling than housework. Soon she found a job in a realty office and responded well to the daily demands.

Before long Randy and Chris pulled up stakes and moved to San Diego to make the most of their new careers.

This story can be repeated millions of times. Unfortunately, half of the families that adopt new lifestyles fall apart. It's to Randy and Chris's credit that they made some personal adjustments as their professional and geographic lives went into contortions. In the midst of rapid shifts they continued to cultivate their love. Randy let boxes sit and took Chris out to dinner. They intentionally moved their conversation from "When will the trucks arrive?" to "How are you feeling?" and "Let's take a Saturday afternoon and drive to the beach."

Neither allowed himself to be buried by things. As the outward part of life changed, they rededicated themselves to their core relationship.

If change causes acute agony in your relationship, you may be experiencing the early stages of burnout. You are tired of adapting, understanding and giving in. You long for peace and predictability. Those are a few hints that you have a problem which must be addressed.

3. Do you feel adequately rewarded?

We all have days when we see ourselves as the boot-scrapers of life; it seems that people constantly are cleaning their mud off on us. It's normal to feel that way once in a while, but if we come to where we seldom think we are rewarded in any way, we begin to feel comatose.

This is easily identified in work situations. In order to work at our peak, we need to feel as though our compensation is reasonable. It doesn't have to be total—that would leave us with nothing to complain about and would seem unnatural. As long as our reward is in the ballpark, though, we are motivated and put in at least an acceptable performance.

When compensation drops below the reasonable mark, employees frequently resort to stealing or to subtle forms of sabotage. Their spirits decline and they become hazardous workers. The same basic principle carries over into marriage. We must feel rewarded.

Notice that the key word in the last sentence is not *rewarded* — it is *feel*. If our partner does not perceive himself as being compensated, he is not.

Therefore, our reward system in marriage must be aimed at our spouse's emotions first of all. Does he feel good about what he is doing and how he is being appreciated? Sensitive couples discern each other's perceptions, and aim at fulfilling them whenever possible.

The Bible presents this in what we could call the "Muzzle-and-Ox Theory." Not to compare our mates with any form of livestock, but the principle is solid. The ox who treads the grain cannot be muzzled in such a way as to prevent him from eating his share of the grain (Deuteronomy 25:4; 1 Timothy 5:18).

It's vital to ask ourselves if we are sure we have not begun to muzzle our marriage. Most often when we do, it is without a formal declaration. Usually we do not even recognize it ourselves, but if we will analyze our behavior, we might notice a shift. For instance,

- Have we begun to make cutting remarks that sound half-way like kidding?

- Do we respond slowly to our responsibilities even though we know it will cause aggravation?

- Have we started dropping out of problem-solving dialog almost as if we were not interested in ameliorating stressful situations?

- Are there times when we think we will benefit by prolonged agitation within the family?

If these and similar scenarios happen more frequently than they used to, we may be trying to complain without knowing how. We feel our needs are not being met but somehow we aren't able to address our grievances. Consequently, we resort to destructive behavior.

The irony is that we would not intentionally hurt our family for anything. We are insulted at the suggestion. Yet the evidence shows that our pain is so great we have ceased trying to help and are now working against ourselves and our family.

To prevent such tragedies, we must maintain an aggressive reward-and-perk system. Words of appreciation, volunteering to help, small gifts and even surprise trips are merely the beginning of adequate compensation. Physical love, evenings out, help with yard work or purchase of a favorite book are only part of a workable pattern.

Couples who are thoughtful enough to acknowledge the numerous good jobs being done are pouring on the fuel to keep the fire burning.

Unfortunately, there are two types of people who make the reward system difficult to operate. **One** is the overly demanding person who only understands huge rewards. He doesn't want to be bothered with small donations. It is extremely difficult to sustain him because his fuel requirements are unreasonable.

The **other** is the one who rejects all rewards. Gifts, signs of appreciation, attempts at affection are all spurned. In effect he has closed the valve and refused to accept fuel. Burning low, he flirts with danger. A person must be balanced enough to be able to handle compliments lest he dry up.

4. *Can you still dream together?*

Dreams are one of the purest forms of fuel. They burn clean and are economical. When we abandon our visions for tomorrow, we reduce ourselves to crude oil and discarded lumber. When we restrict our lives to memories of yesterday and the demands of the present, we shut off one-third of our interests. We shrink our lives to a dull smallness.

Are you able to make short-term goals as well as long-range ones? Do you hesitate to look ahead because of fear of finances, health or job security? Do you turn conversations into diatribes on why you can't do things? If so, you live as a diminished soul, an angel without liftoff.

It would help us to meet Jeff. He always has something on the grill. Among other things, he is now planning ways to assist Indians, is putting together a trip to Colorado, and is devising new toys for children in his neighborhood. For him, to stop dreaming is to cease living.

We all know someone like that and envy him. He has a steady drive and positive spirit, which we long for.

Dreaming is our ticket to hope. It's hard to burn out if we keep reaching together for the dreams we can occasionally whip into reality.

5. *Do you still enjoy people?*

If we find ourselves retreating from people-contacts, we might be giving up. People are a mixed bag, mostly of pleasant encounters but not all. When we start to see people as not worth the bother, we need to be concerned about the direction we are traveling.

If the majority of your relationships remain viable, interesting and enriching, you have little to be concerned about. If you observe them slipping, if you see friends moving or distancing themselves and you lack the energy to rescue or replace them, it's time to set off the alarms.

A great example is Judy. She was divorced, tired, broke and disheveled. Her inclination was to throw in the towel and become a recluse. Yet, she knew better. At considerable risk, Judy refused to go home and die. She forced herself to join groups, bowl, attend church and stay involved in the people network. Her endeavors are paying off.

Marriages receive a great deal of their sparkle from

other people. A couple cannot afford to drain each other continuously as their only source of inspiration. Smart partners keep a sensible flow of people in their lives. Even when it is hard to invite others over or to get out and go places, they make the extra effort to do it. Warm friends are energy suppliers. Your careful collection will help guarantee strength in your relationship.

Take stock of your conversations about others. If the majority of those you know have become "jerks," "dopes," or "slobs," your level of fuel is probably at the bottom of the barrel.

Confronting the Condition

These are only a short selection of touch points where we might get in contact with our present condition. We will examine others in the remainder of the book. However, these samples will acquaint us with the basis of our concern.

We all are capable of burnout in each or any combination of the areas mentioned. When any of them are on the skids, they are bound to hurt the others. There is a lot you can do, though, so there is a lot of hope.

The lady in the Song of Solomon was an incredible optimist. Her fire of love burned so fiercely she was totally convinced that nothing could put it out: It was burning "like a mighty flame. Many waters cannot quench love" (Song of Songs 8:6,7).

Good attitude. Let's put another log on the fire.

Flexercise

---

1. Why do you like being married?
2. How do you feel when you see your partner at the end of a day? Why?
3. What do you see the true condition of your fuel supply to be?

Carryover Burnout

M IKE (MR. NICE GUY) tried his best to get along with everybody. He avoided confrontations, kept his cool and helped his friends, and he was polite to a fault. Unfortunately, his pleasant veneer and suppressed hostility were wrecking his marriage.

When Mike had trouble with his 1982 Ford, he agreed to let his fellow worker, Sid, repair it. Mike wanted to take it to a shop but was reluctant to say no to anyone. Especially since Sid charged so little.

His friend kept the car for two weeks and finally returned it to anxious Mike. The vehicle was pronounced cured and Mike paid Sid, complete with profuse expressions of gratitude. By the time Mike had driven his car home, the knocking had returned and he was angry.

Consistent with his pattern of behavior, Mike complained, wailed, pouted, protested, sulked and ranted. His home life degenerated quickly into a state of maximum stress. In contrast Mike went to work the next day and thanked Sid again for working on his car. At home that evening he continued his tirade over the unrepaired vehicle.

Mr. Nice Guy is typical of abusive partners. He pays almost any price to keep peace when away from the house and expects his partner to absorb his pain when he is at home. His family agonizes enormously through no problem of their own. They suffer unfairly from carryover burnout because he refuses to handle outside conflict.

"But," he argues, "isn't that what a family is for? They are the people you can pour out your feelings to. They are the ones you can count on." It's precisely that attitude that converts the home into a dumping ground. Home is a refueling station of the first tier, but it cannot hope to support all the negatives from every outside activity and still remain solvent. Sometimes families are devastated simply because the members are unwilling to deal with the real sources of burnout.

Where Burnout Comes From

Other times, couples complain that they feel their marriage is drained and they don't know why. Their time together seems tense and exhausting rather than creative, fun and fulfilling. These couples can benefit by making a fuel circle (similar to the one below) to help them discover what areas of their lives are sapping their energy and contributing the most to their burnout.

FUEL CIRCLE

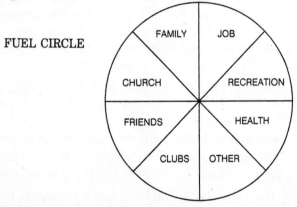

Name the sections of your circle in accordance with your own activities. Then adjust the size of each section to reflect the amount of time you spend in that activity compared with the others. Each circle will be different depending on the couple's interests and activities. Our goal here is to tag the areas of unreasonable fuel drain. Once they are identified, we can plan to adjust them for the sake of energizing our marriages. Can you determine which area is draining an unacceptable amount of your fuel?

The Health Factor

For instance, our casual attitude toward health may have wider consequences than we realize. If we are low on iron, don't get enough sleep, or are going bonkers on caffeine, we are doing more than neglecting our body. We are neglecting our marriage. Indifference to our health draws current from our relationship. Reasonable health maintenance supplies spark.

A typical case of carryover burnout lifestyle is that of Millie, a friend of mine. She wouldn't hurt her family for anything, but by neglecting her body Millie creates an unreasonable strain on her marriage relationship.

Millie stands on her feet and cooks in a restaurant all day. For the past few years she has had back trouble, and being the good soldier (she thinks she is) she refuses to see a doctor or change jobs. So she is tired when she comes home and has reduced her activities to a bare minimum.

If the family wants to go on a picnic or take a trip, Millie naturally sprays chipped ice on everyone's plans. As a result she is seen as the big pain in the family. Everyone slows down or stops entirely to pay homage to Millie's aching back.

She has no incurable disease. A change in routine or medication might help Millie regain her strength and energy. But what difference does it make? After all, it's Millie's back.

That's ridiculous. It's the family's back. By allowing her condition to dull relationships, she hurts everyone. That's equally true of a husband with bad feet or a child with a perpetual cold.

Without being fully aware of our intentions, we may be using our unhealthiness as a tool. We may enjoy dealing with our family from a weakened position, but by remaining a victim of poor health we manipulate our loved ones.

If Millie allows her back to remain in questionable condition, she takes control of the family. When she doesn't want to go someplace, her back is perfect leverage to keep her home. She can use her "condition" to dictate when she and her husband may or may not make love. Should she feel neglected or unappreciated, a few groans about her ailment call immediate attention.

Not every sick person is devious, but too many are. There are reasons we don't take care of ourselves. Could it be that we intentionally hope to drain energy off our marriage? Why would we want to do that?

Health does affect the whole family. When a relatively young husband dies of a condition he could have prevented, the underlying message seems clear: *Why didn't he stop smoking? He didn't care enough about us to take care of himself. If he had, and if he had gone to a doctor, we would still have him here.*

The Job Drain

Maybe we need to check the slice on the fuel circle which indicates our job. Our work might be so boring, unfulfilling, and dead-ended that it turns us into discomforted grouches. Some jobs are distasteful because they demand too much, but not all—some ask little and provide nothing in return.

Day after day listless employees watch the clock and fiddle with their coffee cups. Poorly motivated, these dead-end people are likely to carry their lack of color home. With nothing thrilling going on, they can't talk about hopes, dreams or accomplishments at work. Seldom are we split personalities. If we lead dull, fuel-less lives at work, we usually hold that attitude at home.

Naturally, the job of an overachiever that demands twelve hours a day of frustrating work will rob his marriage of energy. However, the underachiever will puncture his relationship as assuredly as the workaholic. Read that sentence again.

I know a man who studied to be an engineer. He paid the price, took the classes, earned his degree and looked enthusiastically for an exciting job.

Today he works for a large, impersonal company, one where creativity is an ugly word. Every day he drags himself to work and back home again. He takes his check and wishes he were doing something else. Every day! Does it drain off the electricity from his marriage? One guess.

The principle is outlined precisely in Proverbs 15:15: "All the days of the oppressed are wretched, but the cheerful heart has a continual feast."

In other words, if we are getting kicked in the head all day, we are bound to be miserable characters. By moving either the mule or ourselves, however, we could become much happier. As far as possible, we owe it to our spouse to make life a reasonable feast.

The Spiritual Dimension

Many couples are finding that feast in a spiritual commitment. In Nebraska, college football is the number one pastime. The Cornhuskers have furnished exciting shootouts against Oklahoma, U.C.L.A. and Penn State, and in decades of Bowl games.

One of the most successful players at University of Nebraska was explaining two or three years ago where he had been during the fifteen years since he graduated. As the famous running back discussed his career, he added that at one time his marriage had hit the rocks and they knew they needed help.

Along the way, he and his wife became Christians, and since then, their relationship has knitted together, and they have new purpose and commitment.

Their story is the same as that being told by thousands of couples who have made Christ the center of their lives. More about that later.

Good Causes and Harmful Results

Not all of us are locked into dreary situations. Some of us have emotionally bankrupted our marriages because we are pursuing good goals in a destructive manner. Chuck is fanatic over jogging and other recreational activities. He centers his nonworking world on exercise and weight control. Early in the morning he rises and races across parks and over dales. Sunset finds him sucking sunflower seeds and stretching and lifting.

Fanatically, Chuck is chasing noble causes. He looks good, feels good and sports a waistline the size of a sweatband — but his wife is a workout widow. A recreational addict, Chuck burns up his energy day and night and his family suffers the consequences.

When Chuck's wife, Karen, wants to see a movie or take a weekend trip, everything evolves around sit-ups, push-ups and chin-ups. If the motel doesn't have a workout room, if the restaurant doesn't have a granola buffet, Karen can count Chuck out.

That sounds harmless. We might even argue that Chuck is doing something good. But from Karen's viewpoint Chuck appears self-centered and painfully egotistical. His energy is spent at the gymnasium. His creative imagination is dedicated to muscle tone.

Clobbered by Clubs

Some clubs are excellent social outlets, good educational opportunities and often philanthropic endeavors. A number of healthy benefits certainly can be derived from belonging to one or two of these. (Beware, though — a few groups are seedy and apparently exist to reinforce baser instincts like gossip, complaining and prejudice. These you don't need.)

Trouble arises when a club becomes too active and starts cutting into family relationships. However, the fault does not lie entirely with the club. Occasionally we meet someone who wraps himself in the blanket of a club in order to hide from spouse and children. We must draw a line which the organization cannot cross. We are the ones to decide when this tiger is about to eat us.

Staying Calm at Church

We could fill pages with positive things to say about the church, but space dictates that we give just a few suggestions for now. Consider these simple guidelines:

1. Take two jobs at church and say no to the rest. Give your best to one committee and teach one class or study.

2. Let the church buoy your family, not sink it. Don't attend every flute recital and mirror dedication.

3. Ask for instruction on how to strengthen couples and families. Plug these into the existing time slots—don't create more nights out.

Removal of the Crown

Carryover burnout is a predictable shift in most relationships. When we dated, we designated our partner king or queen. We put the crown on his head and served him well. We courted him with regular supplies of gifts, trips, sacrifices, dinners, phone calls and midnight antics. Even if we were broke, we still invested enormous quantities of energy.

Floating on clouds, we dedicated ourselves to impressing and pleasing the person we wanted. As the first year or two of the marriage unfolded, that attitude continued to prevail. We created a life of happy exploration, shared dreams, good conversations and runs through parks while holding hands. Occasionally the relationship suffered a shock, but love overcame.

Sometime between the first and third year, though, we reached over and removed the crown from our lover's head. We can't remember the exact day, maybe there wasn't one, but we definitely dethroned our former monarch.

The pressure of bills, school, relatives, crippled cars, and the probable advent of a child left no room for a reigning king or queen. Life became practical. We made a perceptible shift away from our partner to deal with more pressing issues. Most of us could feel that change even if we chose not to discuss it.

For millions the shift becomes unbearable. That probably explains the sharp rise in divorce during the three-to-five-years-of-marriage period. Not only is he (or she) no longer on the throne, but also the throne is overrun by usurpers, each demanding allegiance.

Soon the wife chooses which tyrants she will serve. Job, school, child, church, or friends. The husband tries to appease the jealous calls of cars, clubs, recreation, friends, career or whatever assortment cries the loudest.

The fires of love burn low because there isn't enough fuel to go around. They have decided to supply energy to the other outlets, and their relationship goes begging. Millions feel it and too many vote to split.

Sadly, most of us don't know what happened. We thought all of our concerns were legitimate. Out of control, we chased every other goal that raised its head while our happy kingdom disintegrated.

The king and queen lost sight of another eternal principle: There is time for everything that needs to be done. The Bible says it this way: "There is a time for everything, and a season for every activity under heaven" (Ecclesiastes 3:1). By shifting priorities and eliminating activities sensibly the king and queen could have kept their crowns. They may have had to settle for a bit less service, but nothing as drastic as they have suffered.

Effective Incentives

These trying conditions are only exaggerated by our refusal to honor relationships. In our nonpersonal society we make position, objects, travel, houses and prestige the benchmarks of a fulfilling life.

Maintaining an acceptable relationship, especially a marriage, brings no tangible prizes as incentives. Since maintenance has become a low goal, fewer of us are willing to sacrifice to nurture our relationships. Marriage has joined the category of the temporal along with clothing, cars and pop cans. We see little point in saving it since it appears to have lost its value.

One summer Pat and I drove from Nebraska to Detroit, Michigan, to see friends. Around Davenport, Iowa, Pat took over the wheel, and I soon fell fast asleep on the passenger side.

Some time later I woke up when we stopped at a rest area on the Everett Dirksen Highway. I had never seen the road referred to as that, but you learn something every day. I got back in the car with a shrug and went back to sleep as Pat drove on.

When I awoke the second time to take my turn at the wheel, I discovered that we were an hour and a half south of Chicago because Pat had misread a sign.

How ticked should a husband be when his wife makes a mistake like that? Honestly, I wasn't angry at all. The first thing that occurred to me was: I could easily have made the same turn. Why become angry over a natural error? And if that isn't enough, we love each other.

Late in the day we kidded about the "scenic route" we had taken. Pat did most of the joking. I remembered that love does not hurt, or seek revenge, or flog. Love understands that we are both cut from the same material and we both get our directions confused.

If a relationship on the job is fractured, we calculate its effect and almost immediately determine that we must mend the break so we can continue our trek toward success. Often marriage does not offer the same motivation, nor does it receive even the same concern. Marriages end regularly, and divorce seems a viable option. We spend the most expensive fuel on the projects we prize the most. The relationships we consider less important receive the crude oil or whatever is left over.

Most of the wall plaques we see are phrases aimed at inspiration and drive. Maybe they should be tempered with this quiet warning:

> *DO NOT WEAR YOURSELF OUT TO GET RICH;*
> *HAVE THE WISDOM TO SHOW RESTRAINT*
> (Proverbs 23:4).

When speaking to groups, I enjoy asking what they have done recently that would qualify as romantic. The response is minimal. Either they are bashful or they have committed few acts of cunning passion. I am afraid most of us have opted for the practical, the immediate, and the ambitious, and we have allowed the romantic fuel tank to run dry or deteriorate to crude oil.

Two Types of Carryover Burnout

To recap, there are two ways to inflict carryover burnout. **One** is to give all of our energies to outside activities and responsibilities. **The other** is to tie ourselves to listless, fruitless jobs all day and come home with little or no hope. The unmotivated life will spill over into our homes, leaving everyone we touch with early signs of coma.

There is a special moment each day when families or couples reunite after fulfilling their separate responsibilities. Paul Welter calls it the regathering.[1] The first thirty seconds of coming together after school or work, he says, set the emotional climate for the evening.

Smart partners try to give something extra when they get home. They do not leave all their energy at the arena. When necessary they get a cup of coffee, eat a couple of crackers and try to collect themselves, realizing that their relationships at home are too important to offer a mere handful of leftovers.

High achievers like Bob are tragic examples of husbands who give all at the office. They are power-packed personalities to the world but sad characters at home.

Bob had gotten himself into a destructive pattern. Every morning he practically screwed a smile onto his face and charged out to face the world. He sold his product, slapped backs, traded jokes and pounded out a living. At night he came home, took off his smile, slumped into the living room chair, sulked, pouted, complained and pampered himself. The next morning he screwed his smile back on and hopped on the treadmill again. His clients got the best Bob; his family, the leftovers.

With a few changes Bob could give part of that pluck to his wife, Jody. He needed to plan his evenings like he organized his day. If Bob ate an apple for perkiness and thought ahead of what Jody needed, he could plug interesting, even exciting evenings into his life at home.

Flexercise

1. Name two areas of burnout that are affecting your relationship with your family.

2. How could you reduce the outside burnout?

3. How does your health affect your family relationships? How could you improve that situation?

1. Paul Welter, *Learning From Children* (Wheaton, IL: Tyndale House Publishers, 1984), p. 147.

*A*djust or *E*xplode

W E DECIDED TO actually program change into our lives," Larry said. He and Shirley had been married for twelve years and they saw it as an adventure. "Each year we have introduced two new elements into our marriage, according to a schedule.

"One year we decided to take up bowling and hiking. Both took time and energy but they added freshness and companionship. Another year we introduced ourselves to square dancing and a Bible study group.

"We can't afford to sink into dullness."

Larry and his wife do not see life as a threat. They have not dug in, waiting for the years to pass quietly. Change is their friend and they treat it well.

Unfortunately, many of us dedicate ourselves to sameness, and we pay a dear price for it. The strain puts our relationship at high risk and it is expensive.

We have heard people explain painfully that they are not the same as they were when they married. At twenty-two our outlook and expectations are different from what they are when we reach thirty-two. By then we are less idealistic, often deep in the process of raising children and in the middle of paying bills on big items.

Since they each have changed and their circumstances are different, many couples want out of marriage. "You've changed, and so have I," is a popular theme, and it leads to a high failure rate.

Different Speeds

Even if we accept the fact that change is inevitable, we must also deal with the fact that it is uneven. Our spouses will almost certainly change in ways different from and at rates other than what we will.

Our energy will come and go and flow at different times. Our interests in sports, reading, camping, serving and working will not keep an even pace with our partner's interests. Since we remain highly individualistic, we have to guard against moving away from the person we love. If our changes are too drastic and in sharply opposite directions, we may wake up married to a stranger.

In a nutshell, here's the problem:

1. Change will come naturally.

2. Change will come individually.

3. Change can drive us apart.

and the solution:

We must become the controller and create constructive change so that we do not become victims of the imbalance of uncontrollable changes.

Balanced Change

Most of our significant changes have been imposed on us. Responsibility, routine, and regrets are three horsemen who rule our lives.

All of us suffer when change is imposed. We can't avoid the natural demands of life, but we can balance uncontrollable change by making some planned changes of our own that we would like, some controlled changes.

Good change sometimes comes serendipitously. You can Thank God, kiss your mailman, throw pizza in the air when the surprise arrives, but you can't beat *planned change* for a dependable upbeat. And upbeat is so healthy for us we dare not leave it to mere chance.

Those who take a reasonable amount of control over the changes in their lives are more likely to produce a happy marriage. Got that? How about reading it again?

In a biblical context, James says this about control: "Or take ships as an example. Although they are so large and are driven by strong winds, they are steered by a very small rudder wherever the pilot wants to go" (3:4). Creative change becomes our rudder, guaranteeing that we exercise control over where this ship of marriage is going.

In a slower world, a couple could have married and expected little change over their forty- to fifty-year union. What you saw was often what you got—and kept. Not so today. The most dependable characteristic of your marriage may be the inevitability of its change. Children, career, mobility, divorce, death, job flexibility—all these almost guarantee that things will not continue as they are.

Chart of Change

MAIN EVENTS	STRESS FACTORS
First married (stress and pleasure)	Turbulent highs—good, bad, confusing. High sexual activity. Personal adjustment.
Introduction of children (couple's relationship often redefined; big demands, little money)	Happiness—limiting, boring, exciting. Burdensome and great appreciation. *High risk.* Rapid change.
Raising children	Pleasant years often controlled by needs of children. School centered. Building career, home, social life.
Topping off teenagers	Rapid change in teens can be stimulating to parents. Painful, rewarding.
Personal readjustment (rough road at first)	*High risk.* Can no longer hide behind children. Opportunity to fall in love all over again.

Grandparenting (enjoyable years)	If health holds, could be best years of life. Mellowing.
Retirement (re-readjustment; health stress)	Cannot hide behind job. If interests are mutual and health is good, can be highly rewarding.
Twilight (relaxed; some health problems; frequently appreciate each other)	Those who stay active seem most fulfilled and happy.

Try not to be shocked by change. With an idea of what to expect you will not be knocked off your carpet. Other issues such as extended family and economics will contribute, but these groups will provide a framework.

Good Change and Bad

Young people often imagine that good changes will bring more happiness and a closer relationship. They also picture hardships such as job loss, poor health and earthquakes as tearing them apart. Older people know better.

Good events are great, but they are the ones that catch us unaware. Upward mobility is frequently rapid movement, and you may not be prepared for the sudden acceleration.

Conventional "wisdom" tells us you can't have too many good things happen to you. But you can. Especially if you don't have time to retool. Rapid and multiple changes are like sudden currents that can sweep our feet out from under us.

So keep an eye on the job advancement. Be ready to adjust to a new car. To avoid this couple's problem, prepare yourself for the move into a wealthier neighborhood:

Ed said, "Cindy just wasn't ready to travel at my speed. When I became vice president that meant more parties, entertaining and nights out. She enjoyed the added money but wasn't able to take what went with it."

The Female Factor

Few areas in society are moving as fast as the change in female roles. The steady but sure rise of women into managerial and leadership positions has introduced new dynamics into marriage relationships as well. Couples now need to plan for and allow stretch for that expansion.

One couple I visited insisted they had thoroughly discussed the implications of her career. Although Jim came from a conservative background, he agreed to make the sacrifices necessary for June's job. They talked it over before their marriage, as any smart couple should.

After their first year, June's job became more complicated. She began to make business trips, worked an occasional evening and often brought papers home to finish. As her responsibilities grew, Jim's patience shrank. He stared more, talked less. When he did speak, his sentences were short and accusatory.

By the second year Jim and June had a genuine crisis on their hands. What Jim had promised before the wedding was different from what he could now deliver.

Change had brought painful friction. As quickly as possible they needed to talk, plan, reorganize and compromise. By adjusting they had an excellent chance of avoiding a full-blown explosion. Fortunately, they each had enough love to make both of them want to work it out.

Quick Check

When drastic change comes, you *must* talk. Asking yourselves some of the following questions may help get your discussion off to an encouraging start.

1. How long will this change last?
2. What is the up-side for each of us?
3. What is the down-side for each of us?
4. How can we mitigate the down-side?

5. What would be the loving action for each of us?

6. In what creative ways can we turn these changes to benefit our marriage?

Use these questions for starters, and then add others that are more pointed to your situation.

Xenophobia

One of our greatest fears is the fear of change. Called *xenophobia,* this malady often afflicts the extremely insecure. In their search for security, they dig a deep hole and try desperately to crawl in and stay put.

Anything that seems foreign to them is suspect. The same mentality that asks, "Do you know any other churches that do this?" translates it in marriage to, "Do you know any other couples who use this system?"

Blessed be the spirit of constructive change.

Flexercise

1. What is the biggest change you have faced so far in your marriage? How did you handle it?

2. What changes are you presently putting into your relationship?

3. What changes would you like to suggest to your mate? Why don't you?

*C*heck *Y*our *E*xpectations

GENE LOVED TO make plans. He spent many evenings at home, papers spread across the table, penciling out his future. Tirelessly, he calculated finances, investments and pensions. When he wasn't poring over checkbooks, he was unfolding maps and dreaming of trout streams.

It was important for Gene to know where he was going and imperative that he know how to get there. Meanwhile, his wife, Mary, stood by and let him do his thing.

Unfortunately, what Gene was trying to do for them was slowly stretching them apart. He wanted Mary to trust him and he in turn would relieve her of the agony of decision making. Instead of feeling secure, Mary suffered from the creeping jitters. The less information she had, the more she was left out of the process, and the greater was her nervous rash.

"Part of it was my own problem," she explained. "I know I don't like to make decisions, but I soon found that the sense of being left out of your own future is terrifying."

To reduce her tension, Mary needed for them to discuss their goals together, agree on those goals, and share in reaching them. Gene is including her more now, rather than just letting her sit by and wait to see what he is going to do next.

Balanced couples have three interlocking sides to their goal setting. They are: short-term goals, long-term goals, mutual goals.

GOALS

Without these three elements, a couple's relationship can hurt from lack of well-rounded expectations. Any relationship without reasonable mutual anticipation risks the possibility of failure. All three types of goals are important to maintaining a sense of balance. We grow as we meet short-term goals. We need to defer some of our dreams until next year or when the children are grown, or when we retire, but our enthusiasm and excitement strengthens our marriage and our joy in each other remains fresher when we realize some of them together as we go along.

Short-term Goals

Each of us must have plans for today and next week and next month. We cannot stumble from day to day waiting to see what pops up. However, neither can we afford to lay up all of our bricks for the distant future. If all of our gratifications are delayed or suspended, we end up with a dull, boring now, in favor of an "iffy" tomorrow.

Short-term goals put a couple on top of where they want to be. Going out for coffee, playing tennis, having friends over, and enjoying good sex are all part of keeping short accounts. Our labor needs to be followed shortly by small, reassuring rewards. "Hope deferred makes the heart sick" (Proverbs 13:12).

Long-term Goals

Five or ten years down the road we will want to know what we have accomplished. Saving for the trip, the car, tendency is to major on one of these. Some of us are either all short-term or all long-term. By being entirely microscopic or entirely telescopic, we lose the satisfaction of the one we ignore. Long term we are looking for the big prizes. Life must consist of more than coffee and walks in the park. By putting aside for the house, the trip to France, or a year of volunteer work, we avoid hand-to-mouth gratification as our sole reward. The total picture allows us to make sacrifices now so we will find even greater fulfillment later.

By mapping out the long term, we greatly increase the possibility of reaching our destination. Most people who see Paris took time to plan on how to get there.

Mutual Goals

If either partner is void of ambition or dreams, the other mate is obligated to fill in the gap. That isn't fair. Care what happens to you. Care today. Care tomorrow. When only one person has goals, the relationship is often unbalanced. Unbalanced relationships run terrible risks over the long haul.

The best way to resolve separate goals is to come to each other with broad guidelines and begin to narrow them together. Discussion openers like, "How would you like to take a trip this winter?" could get the conversation rolling. Statements like, "I talked to the travel agent about going fishing in Alaska on May 15," doesn't leave much room for reaching a happy compromise.

When our partner brings us a goal or searches out a plan, try not to dump on him or on her ideas. If our spouse gets the ice water treatment every time, he might give up making suggestions. Be positive. Look for ways to help your partner's dreams come true and do it in a manner that will leave both of you grinning like bears at a beehive.

Clusters of Expectations

Many of us fail to understand our goals and thus have little chance of fulfilling them. If we allow our expectations to be free-floating and vague, we are far less likely to achieve them. Couples need to brainstorm and bring their lives into focus.

Focusing is a three-step process:

1. List what you want.

2. Cluster your wants according to priorities.

3. Plan to make each a reality.

Your list may consist of a number of different goals including career, home, relationships, money, vacation, time with children, education, spiritual life, etc.

Having compiled your list, cluster the goals according to priority. Clusters are better than lists because you probably don't have a first, second or third priority. More likely you have two or three number one priorities.

Your clusters may look something like this:

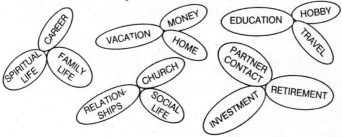

Don't necessarily copy these clusters; don't take your own clusters too literally; and definitely do not make them yours alone. Go to the pleasant effort of evaluating your lives together as a couple as you create your clusters.

Take the time to discuss each priority specifically in each cluster. If spiritual life, family life and career are to prosper in the first cluster, how do you plan to bring that about? Spiritual life may take: (1) buying a study guide you both can use; (2) cutting out a specific time to get alone or together; and (3) deciding to read through the psalms in three months or the Bible in one year. Stay flexible, but try to spell it out. *The last thing you want to do is regiment life to death.* Think out how your goals can be accomplished and come to a reasonable agreement.

Hang loose! Some priorities will overlap. Others will be in the wrong cluster. Next year you will want to move one or two up or down. No problem. Make them fit yourselves.

People who have no concept of their expectations often find themselves entangled in the wrong project for too long. They spend hours on their lawn and minutes with their children. They devote themselves to their hobbies and never get promoted in their jobs. They throw themselves at the moment and fail to prepare for the future.

After your clusters are organized in fairly good shape, plan your method of attack on each. How will you reach each goal? It's like having four piggy banks: one for pennies, one for nickels, one for dimes and one for quarters. You put coins into their proper banks regularly, and each grows steadily. Clusters of expectations will grow with the same dependability.

An over-the-road truck driver looked at his clusters and decided he had them in the wrong groups. Truck driving gave him freedom and a respectable income. It allowed him to escape the confines of the factory and made him feel like an open-ended cowboy. However, his job placed his children, wife and church into a lower cluster.

He was achieving what he wanted, but not what he wanted most. A look at his expectations and priorities inspired him to reevaluate his job. By creating a form of clusters the truck driver could see which areas of his life should share importance with his career. From there he could start to pull in the significant parts that were left begging.

Missing Goals/Goals Missing

I have great respect for women who work at home, but I realize that some suffer from a degree of disorientation.

Most housewives have trouble knowing whether they are winning or losing. Since their work is literally never finished, they cannot sit down and say, "There, I've done it." There are always more chores, always different tasks to do. Without having well-defined boundaries these women often lead lives of considerable frustration.

A housewife could start the day with a realistic list of five things she wants to accomplish. A list of twenty things that need to be done in the house is unrealistic and frustrating. Narrow your goals. When you reach the fifth goal, throw up your hands and sing hallelujah. You've had a great day. Tomorrow you can do another five.

A couple lacking boundaries is condemned to the same madness. How do they know if they are out of whack? How do they know which arrow is missing its mark if they have only a vague idea of where they are aiming?

Peggy said, "We were never going to be content with a dull life. We were going to 'do something.' But after all these years we still sit around because we can't decide what 'do something' means."

Ted's story is just as sad. He knew what he wanted to do. He wanted to spend time with his son, Tony. In his mind Tony was always on top. Nothing seemed more important. Unfortunately, Ted kept shoving Tony down to the wrong cluster. Ted's goals and his reality were far apart. Like millions of other fathers, he woke up one day and realized he had a high school boy he barely knew.

Every couple has frustrated expectations. That's part of the normal rat race. But missing some of your goals is a far cry from not taking aim at any targets.

To have a thousand goals is to have none. To dream of a thousand trips is to stay home. To talk about a thousand plans is to accomplish nothing. That's why we cluster.

Strong Families Share Goals

Since the average child has little or no concept of what

his father does at work, it's obvious that many of us share few of our dreams and goals with our families. What does our spouse find particularly satisfying or highly frustrating about his job? Often we resemble satellites, each swinging out into our own orbits and having little to do with one another.

Imagine that your family sat down together and discussed the program. Why do we live here? What would mother and father like to accomplish with their jobs? Why do we attend the church we do? What would we really like to buy and how much would we have to save each payday for how long to get it?

By sharing dreams with our family, we create a group that pulls together rather than strains apart.

Everyone wants to feel that he is a necessary component of his family. He wants to know that if anything happens to him, a hole would exist in the family that no one else could fill. A family's sense of oneness is greatly enhanced when each member is included in the planning and working out of family goals.

The days when Dad could come home and announce to a startled family, "Pack up; we're moving to Pittsburgh," are over. Today, each member must become a part of the process as early as possible. He must be kept abreast of developments. Each must feel that his needs and preferences have been considered fully. If we are not given time and consideration, we are less able to adapt to the idea of moving. By being made to feel like a useless pawn, we will fail to pitch in and give emotional support. Crack the door. Let everyone know a move is a possibility. Allow everyone to express any misgivings and get them out in the open. Maybe there are circumstances we have not weighed.

Given time, each member of the family could begin to see the benefits of making the move.

A great deal can be said about the value of spontaneity. Many families are too structured; they are almost afraid of any sudden impulse or fresh breeze. The most satisfying place is probably somewhere in the middle. We need to go for the moment, but at the same time take good measure of what tomorrow holds.

Flexercise

1. What would you like to accomplish with your spouse during the next year?

2. Have you clustered your goals? If not, this is the time.

3. What three goals did you put into your first cluster? How are you progressing toward those aims?

Everyone Else Is Hang Gliding

HERE'S OUR THOUGHT for today: What happens if you put a chameleon on a plaid sports coat? Will the little lizard explode trying to match all the colors?

Now consider this: What happens if a couple looks around and tries to make their marriage like all the other marriages they see? Does the couple twist into a pretzel?

The answer is easy. We do become distorted when we try to pattern ourselves after others. It's a mathematical principle. The more we try to be like others, the less content we are to be ourselves, and the less happy we will be.

Look at it as an equation:

Trying to be like others	+	Being less like ourselves	=	Unhappiness with ourselves

A couple from Oregon told me, "We used fashion catalogs to plan our lives. If it was in, we had to have it. We were living above our heads and we knew it. But we couldn't bear the thought that our friends had better cars or larger boats.

"We drove hard to have it all. Relationships meant little to us. It's a wonder our marriage survived." Fortunately, God woke them up to the fact that people and their love for each other were more important than fads or trends.

Arrested Adolescence

You can see the problem clearly among adolescents. Busy trying to establish their own identities, teenagers look at cheerleaders, football players, honor students, drinkers, car fans—all the time trying to discover where they fit in and who they are. We expect that kind of scrambling during those years and we don't worry too much about it, but if the same type of feelings carry over into marriage, there is reason for concern.

Many of our problems do linger from high school. For some, social acceptance is of urgent importance. Do we go to the right parties, wear the correct clothes, drive the good cars? Do we fit into the right crowds? We quiver over the question of finding worth in the proper setting.

Ten years later the same search to "belong" may continue to control our lives. Twenty, thirty or forty years later it could still be dictating our lifestyle. We still dream of being invited to the right parties, attending prestigious weddings or serving on committees that will "establish our identity."

Instead of trying to fulfill our youthful dreams, we need to appreciate maturity. It is an honor to become an adult and live in the present. Those who accept the pleasures and challenges of growing up no longer need to make sacrifices to the cult of adolescence-past.

There are three aspects of this problem that are bound to put too much strain on a marriage:

1. A hapless search for identity

We need to feed our marriage with a certain amount of self-contentment. Never knowing who we are, what we are like or where we are going saps our marriage of vital energy.

2. A restless sense of jealousy

Marriage cannot be healthy if you live with your nose in your neighbor's garbage can. The more we check to see what others are eating, drinking, wearing or reading, the more we are hindered from giving ourselves to each other.

3. *A desire to be someone else*

Some women still want to be like movie stars. That may have been reasonable at twenty-two, but at forty-two it is probably wasted dreaming. That's different from goal setting. Goal setting establishes a level you would like to reach and one which is reasonably possible. Sounds perfectly sane. But it's another matter if that goal is to become another person.

Worst of all is a feeling of free-floating envy. That means the targets keep moving. We think we want to be like Mrs. Johnson. When we get close to being like her, we switch to wanting to be like Mrs. Jones.

Trying to be like someone else is a poor goal. Aiming to be like everyone else is a cruel ambition.

The solution to each of these dilemmas is found in becoming calm at the core. We become thankful for who we are and thankful for who we married. We want to work at being excellent at who we are instead of wishing we were someone else.

Calmness at the core prevents us from chasing after foolish goals and pretense. We want the freedom to be ourselves. "Calmness can lay great errors to rest" (Ecclesiastes 10:4).

Wise people narrow the target to themselves alone. Unable to be everyone else, we put our own picture in the middle of the bull's eye and hit it squarely.

Two Essential Questions

It would be interesting to ask any group of married couples two questions.

One, how many of you have ever gotten yourselves into financial trouble trying to live the lifestyle of others? That is, buying vans, purchasing cottages, taking up skiing, or going on cruises because other people do it.

Two, how many of you have argued and felt pain in your relationship because you over-extended trying to keep up with the Joneses? That is, you felt strong tension because you had trouble agreeing on how far to venture out and spend in order to do the "in" thing.

We might be surprised at how many people have experienced unnecessary agony simply because they have chased someone else's dreams.

Not that vans, cottages and other things are evil or extravagant. The key is to keep them within our own tastes, our own finances and our own timing. When we are stable and confident, we are able to travel at our own speed. The less mature can get caught up in allowing others to set the pace and beat the drum.

Rotten Bones

While looking for special formulas that might enhance our marriages, we sometimes miss the basics. The simple disease of envy will do as much to wreck a marriage as any other intrusion. The author of Proverbs is helpful, even with his bluntness: "Envy rots the bones" (14:30).

Envy and jealousy threaten the heart of any relationship. If we envy things, it is easy to envy people also. We want their van, we want their cottage, we want their wife. That may explain partly why God warns us against panting over our neighbor's collection of goodies (Exodus 20:17).

The couple who have learned contentment do not gnaw away at life wishing they were someone else. Instead, they strive for their own goals, take risks and rise up to meet the challenges of tomorrow—together.

Happy couples catch the wind in their own time and sail the seas for themselves.

Customized and Personalized

Any dip can try to copy his lifestyle, dreams and hopes from some person on television or in the movies. Any tick can let his neighbors tell him how to live. Be caring enough to carve out the expectations that you and your family will honestly find satisfying.

Take this pledge and say it twice:

> # We will never be content to settle for someone else's goals.

The spiritual world is an essential part of our daily existence. Our goals will not be entirely selfish because we live in touch with Christ's will for us and for those we contact.

With that in mind, you can take a second pledge:

> # Our goal-setting will be satisfying to God.

So we make it our goal to please him, whether we are at home in the body or away from it (2 Corinthians 5:9).

Flexercise

1. Which is more important, your lifestyle or your relationships? Why?

2. What have you done for yourselves lately that is different from what the crowd around you does?

3. What are you now involved in that you consider to be working toward a spiritual goal?

Rewards and Perks

H AVE YOU EVER WORKED where the staff was seriously underpaid? It is not unusual to feel deprived, but it hurts terribly if you run grievously short. Eventually something has to give.

Signs begin to appear, such as poor morale, missing product, slowed production or absenteeism. If left unaddressed, employee turnover is soon noticeable. Good people leave and less capable workers take their places.

Similar symptoms appear in marriages where one or both parties feel inadequately compensated. Everyone expects to get something out of marriage. We don't tie knots simply to see how much we can give. A few expect very little in return, but even they must see a payday from time to time.

Some of the common complaints we hear are: "I never get my way"; "I'm giving in 90 percent of the time"; and, "When we make love, he never takes time for me." These people are saying they contribute to the relationship but are poorly paid in return.

Everyone has a right to compensation. It is even more significant that he needs to *feel* compensated. He may be getting gigantic benefits but it doesn't do him much good unless he has a clear sense of their value to him. Possibly, he is receiving the wrong pay for him. The person may want and need apples when he is getting oranges. On the other hand, he may have no idea what he wants, or he may be expecting far too much.

Let's briefly consider each of these possibilities:

Expecting Gigantic Benefits

Mary entered marriage with her eyes tightly closed. Television had been her marriage manual and Southfork was her dollhouse. She connected with an outstanding husband, but unfortunately he couldn't make her happy. High debts and huge mortgages only proved to be yeast for the greater things she wanted.

It wasn't that Mary was evil; she simply was unrealistic. Her failure to deal with the facts left her incapable of enjoying the excellent rewards she had.

Husbands often enter marriage equally unrealistic. Some expect an impossible level of servitude from their wives.

Couples in this fairyland need a frank discussion about practical compensation. They may quickly realize how well off they are. Their rewards from being married are outstanding, and they are fortunate when they learn to appreciate them.

To reach a healthy sense of rewards we need to share our dreams with others. Bible study groups can help us see values as God sees them. Discussion with others about giving, helping, even sacrificing will tend to keep our ship on a sure course. None of us can afford to let this world shape our value system.

Receiving the Wrong Pay

It's frustrating to live with someone who thinks he knows what you need. Since he knows everything, he has no need to listen. He buys blenders for a wife who doesn't want them and plans vacations to cities she hates. She cooks food that gags her partner.

They do everything except the right thing. Spending money and energy, they miss the mark most of the time. Unfortunately, that doesn't deter them since they each think they know what is best for the other.

Too often, when she is longing for a warm hug and a few kind words, he works like a three-armed paperhanger to compensate with objects, things and events. "Let's buy something, go somewhere." He simply is shopping in the wrong store.

Sincere communication with lots of close listening would solve most of this frustration — and be cheaper in the long run.

Not Knowing Himself

This one is a special curse. You can hug her, buy her flowers, make popcorn, rent an old movie, beat the rugs, sing in the rain in the town square, and she will barely crack a smile.

She never professes to want or need anything. Thoroughly frustrated, her partner beats his brains out attempting the impossible.

People like this do exist, and they are playing dirty pool. They owe it to their partners to develop some 'druthers. Many times they are suffering from poor self-image and don't believe they deserve anything. If this is the case, they also owe it to their partners to get some counseling. It can set them free to be themselves, to develop their own true personalities, and to discover what they really do or don't want. If you are an apathetic spouse, for the sake of your marriage, create a wish list, emotional and physical, and let your partner in on it.

Everyone enjoys Kirk and Tanya. They never ruffle anyone's feathers. In ten years of marriage they have demanded little and seldom argued. That's their problem.

When Kirk and Tanya go out for supper, they frequently spend the evening frustrated. Kirk will ask Tanya where she would like to eat. She replies limply that she doesn't care. "Any place is fine with me."

That kind of wimping-out bothers Kirk. She never has a preference and he translates that as not really wanting to go to a restaurant. In turn, Kirk doesn't want to pick a place for fear he is being too domineering.

So both end up wimping out. More than once this couple has circled the town and driven home. Neither wants to take a stand and say, "I want to eat at Wally's." Under the guise of kindness they strain their relationship until it is often too painful to have an evening out.

Our partners have a right to know what we want. That's basic to a satisfactory reward system.

The Genuinely Content

We need to take note here that there is a rare but blessed group of partners who do feel perfectly compensated. Generally they like the way things are going and when adjustments are necessary, they lovingly speak up. They can handle hard knocks in their relationship, but they refuse to be run over.

These happy spouses can miss a paycheck from time to time, but they don't let the quartermaster get too far in arrears. Neat, tight accounting keeps both members of the corporation happy.

Reasonable Benefits

Each of us can enrich our marriage by facing the issue of rewards squarely. Compensation, rewards and perks are benefits that reasonably can be expected from a marriage union. Speaking of the virtuous woman, Proverbs says: "Give her the reward she has earned, and let her works bring her praise at the city gate" (31:31).

Having recognized the role of rewards in marriage, let's identify what constitutes adequate compensation for ourselves. Later, we will discuss pay for our partner.

Begin modestly. Save the villa in the south of France for a later list. Each of you write down eight rewards you would cherish in your relationship, and then discuss them together. The following are mere suggestions:

gratitude	night out
set the table	walks in the park
phone calls	clothing allowance
conversation	single stem rose
bedtime	trip to the beach
turn TV off	Sunday football

It's only a start. Later you might devise an additional list or revise this one. Now you are communicating rather than guessing.

This also places the question of compensation in both laps. You each describe what you expect. Each partner in turn must deliver the goods.

The lists could be magnetized to the refrigerator unless they are too graphically intimate. No matter where the notes are kept, at least the gap has been bridged and hope runs higher. Possibly for the first time in your married life you will have a fairly good idea of what each of you expects.

Jackie Gleason's *Honeymooners* gives us a great example of the difference between salary, rewards and perks in marriage. Ralph believes Alice should be thrilled to receive a basic salary for being married to him. The salary she gets is an apartment, food and the pleasure of his company. He considers a television set, a telephone and a car extravagances that she doesn't need. In his mind Alice should be happy to remain inside the bare walls he refers to as "the lap of luxury." Rewards and perks are out of the question to this Neanderthal husband, who rules out trips, education, a romantic evening, goal setting, and creative dreaming.

While most of us have stretched beyond this caveman

relationship, we may not have gone far. If the only things we get out of marriage are the bare bones of existence, our partnership is at risk. The sheer boredom of a routine marriage is enough to kill it.

Dealing With Dullness

One couple, Lee and Kim, woke up one dawn to face the dullness of their subsistence marriage. They had given all of their resources to raising children and only a meager pittance was left for themselves. They enjoyed no rewards or perks because they considered it selfish to put themselves first in any way.

They faced the reality that after their children were gone, they would have to live with each other. Frankly, neither knew if he was prepared for that.

Consciously, Lee and Kim began to develop a reward and perk system. They planned trips together, started bowling, set aside times for sex, took classes and played bridge.

They did not neglect the duties of their relationship, but rather they rose above them and branched out to find more gratification. It wasn't easy after years of dull routine, and they tended to drift back, but Lee and Kim fought their regression. Their marriage gained new vitality when they saw its demands and reached beyond them.

The Empty Nest

We are aware of the empty nest syndrome. What do we do when the children leave? Sadly, many parents remain emotionally tethered to them even after they have grown. The few charges they get come from visits with their grandchildren.

If that sounds pleasant enough, consider the consequences. This means the couple is seldom charged because most grandchildren do not live close. Even those who are near have only so much time and energy to share with their gray-templed grandparents. This also means that the parents of the grandchildren face an unreasonable responsibility—they become the source of their parents' vitality and interests. If they sense this role, the duty of supporting their parents emotionally can become burdensome.

Balanced couples ask for only a moderate amount of strength from their children and grandchildren. They continue to receive the major part of their rewards from each other and their own circle of interests.

A Four-Star Pay Scale

Pick yourself as the paymaster and ask what kind of compensation you are handing out. At the same time calculate how long it is between paydays. It may help to grade yourself on the following four-star scale.

———

Praise, reinforcement, compliments, reassurance. A huge number of people have trouble saying, "I love you." They must break the barrier and express feelings of affection. Too many marriage partners starve themselves and their partners emotionally. How many stars do you rate here?

Emotional Pay   *   *   *   *

———

Practically every story we have heard about the benefits of touching are true. We can change our partner, make him feel younger, healthier and more optimistic simply by touching him. Physically deprived spouses tend to retard. Where does this leave you?

Physical Pay   *   *   *   *

———

Do you provide opportunities for discussion? Millions of us are content to watch talk shows and appreciate the conversation of others. Is there plenty of flex time for each partner to verbally express himself?

Conversational Pay   *   *   *   *

———

Each partner needs a designated amount of disposable income to spend on himself without being accountable. It cannot be limitless, but within certain boundaries it must be entirely his. Financial liberty is essential to maintaining a free spirit. How do you rate?

Financial Pay   *   *   *   *
_____

There is no better investment than planning a happy future. A cruise of Alaska, a new set of candleholders, a move to another state will do wonders for one's outlook. Spirits shrivel if they cannot reach into tomorrow. Do your spirits reach four stars?

Dream Pay   *   *   *   *
_____

Self-esteem will skyrocket if the person feels someone cares what he thinks. Often one spouse does most of the talking, leaving the other to feel useless and ignorant. Smart couples aim for equal time and mutual respect. How many stars do you get?

Opinion Pay   *   *   *   *
_____

Each partner deserves a reasonable amount of time to himself. Some couples prosper by being together all of the time, but most do not. The freedom to pursue individual goals is essential to feelings of accomplishment and self-satisfaction. Where are you here?

Open Time Pay   *   *   *   *
_____

The list could go on. Other payments may be appropriate to your situation. How well do you pay the person with whom you share your marriage? How well does your partner pay you?

If we do not feel appreciated or compensated or exhilarated or accomplished, we will reach out to feel something. We stay only so long in limbo. If positive gratification does not eventually arrive, we normally will seek negative compensation. We must feel something to know we are alive. If we have trouble feeling happy, we will soon try to be sad. It hurts too much to feel nothing.

If nothing good happens, we soon will make something bad happen. Usually the unrewarded partner will cause trouble because his needs have not been addressed.

Well-managed marriages depend on a reward system. The partners provide settings to discuss payment schedules. They make the payments regularly. Periodically they review the scale and make adjustments accordingly.

Flexercise

1. Name two things you wish your partner would do for you.
2. How do you reward or pay your spouse?
3. What added bonus could you give?

Explain
Your Low Points

W HEN WE COME HOME tail dragging, jaw rigid, shoulders slumped, breathing fire, the family has a right to know why. It's hard to deal with a dragon.

It's all right for us to be a dragon once in a while. That's a privilege accorded human beings. We all go half crazy now and then. When we absolutely have to, it's fine to come home and fall apart. Given the chance, our family usually responds with emotional first aid and soon we are nursed back to stability. Some of us, however, abuse the right and turn into animals more frequently than necessary.

The particularly painful part of dragon-healing is playing twenty questions trying to find out what is wrong. You've hit the skids and people rush in to offer comfort only to get burned for being near you. Quickly they try to guess what caused the affliction. Did you have an accident? Get fired? Did the kids hide your bowling ball? Did someone call you a nerd?

Discerning What's Wrong

Danny came home to be greeted with a barely audible grunt from his wife Angie. Wanting to be responsive to an obvious need, he sat next to her on the couch. Tension packed the room like a hot air balloon.

"Is anything wrong, honey?" he asked timidly.

"No!" she barked.

He began to play twenty questions with someone hostile. Is it fish? Fowl? Is it bigger than a breadbasket? Does it like to eat mandrake leaves?

Danny hates to have to drag the dragon out of Angie. After the fifth question Danny huffs off to the garage to pound nails on his workbench.

Both know it isn't fair. Worse, the silence is destructive. He feels like rust wondering what he did. She feels like a heel for lashing out at the person who really loves her.

We at least need to announce the category that has sent us tumbling. A simple statement like, "The boss is an idiot," could help clear the air. Even, "I can't find my bowling ball," will give him something to work with. The problem may not go away but it will free up the guiltless so he can respond with appropriate behavior. It may at the same time identify the guilty.

Our initial statement could take one of these four forms:

1. "It's the boss's fault. Give me ten minutes alone."
2. "It's the boss's fault. Here's what he did."
3. "It's the boss's fault. Order a pizza."
4. "It's the boss's fault. Help me think this through now."

The first statement declares a fact and asks for a bit of breathing room. We aren't asking for intervention, only patience for a few minutes.

Statement two defines the problem and asks for a sympathetic ear. We don't want much more than to get it off our chest and receive a pinch of understanding.

Number three explains the situation and asks for relief. She might ask us to put the cat out, start dinner, get her a cup of coffee. It's possible to supply a parachute by contributing some action. If such information isn't forthcoming, we might volunteer, "Is there something I could get you?"

The fourth pronouncement suggests that she is approaching the panic stage. She wants help in sifting this through before she crashes and can't think. Possibly she wants us to help her reason soundly again. Maybe she needs us to reaffirm her worth. She might want to hear some options so she can see light at the end of the tunnel. She might welcome some verbal or maybe physical intervention.

Each of us could add to the list but these should set us calculating. How do you feed a dragon? We ask for a few clues. She owes us that. We then respond by supplying the nutrition that the person calls for. As it becomes a cooperative effort, we can avoid unnecessary drain and frustration.

Acceptable Communication

One gigantic help would be to find a civilized way to say, "My chemistry is off." It takes some partners twenty years to find a graceful way to say they don't feel well. They spend years getting rubbed across a cheese grater simply because they have no acceptable vocabulary.

Don't you love couples who have been married for thirty years? Fred will say, "Martha, I've been constipated all day." Pure poetry. When we are first married, we can't say that. We merely sit across the table looking cross-eyed while our partner tries to guess what's tormenting us.

We are better off if we can speed up the maturing process.

There ought to be a law in every household that when a woman is feeling bad because of her menstrual period she *must* tell her husband. Failure to report should result in a penalty of baking six pies in a week.

Women are often great during the difficult time of the month. But some times are tough. The chipper, perky wife can suddenly turn into a hermit crab and we may not know why. Don't force your husband to figure out what's going on. A short, "Treat me gently, I'm having my period," could save days of agony. If that seems too blunt, make up a signal or a euphemism that you have previously discussed. "These are my down days," or "I'll be a little slow from now till Monday." Whatever words or codes work best for a couple are acceptable—but communication is essential.

The same is true of husbands. Our days may not be as predictable, but they are as real. Sometimes our chemistry fails to balance and we simply don't feel well. Smart husbands tell their wives instead of trying to play charades.

One of the lowest points in marriage is the desolate feeling that "I can't win." It comes after a partner believes he has tried over and over to please the person he loves. He has done the other person's job, bought a present, given up his dreams for the evening, and still the dragon is not tamed. It's burnout time. They have nothing else to offer.

A few well-placed words could prevent this type of thing. Those who are put into a continuous malaise of "I can't win" live under unacceptable strain. We owe it to our partner to reduce these times.

Time Out

When we first got married, I didn't practice time out. I wanted to resolve our low points immediately. I had to win. It could be called "Tear the Door Down Now" therapy. My wife was pouting and I was going to put an end to it. I would try to make things happen. It's a miracle we survived.

Eventually I discovered that she needed a breather. Time out plays a large role in keeping a marriage fresh. The person who is suffering must call for a recess. The partner might give it voluntarily, but don't count on it. I must raise my hand and announce it for myself.

When necessary we have the right to take that time

and retreat in order to regroup. If we choose that, no one has the right to tear our door down. We are asking for time and space to heal, to re-evaluate, and to regain our strength. That could take ten minutes or a weekend. Because we love each other, we ask for a truce. Because we love each other, we grant it.

We ask God to "hide me in the shadow of your wings" (Psalm 17:8). Maybe we ask our spouse to hide us in the shadow of his wings. We take our time out.

Pointing to the Fire

Imagine a city with an excellent fire alarm system. When a fire breaks out, bells ring, firemen whistle down their poles and trucks race from the firehouse. They have everything: trained personnel, modern equipment, total dedication.

The only thing missing is that the dispatcher didn't tell them where the fire is. Frantically they chase down one street and then another. Bouncing across intersections, their eyes search the buildings for smoke, flames, screaming people—any clue as to the location.

Our marriage partner knows there is a fire. Normally an aura surrounds the person who is deep in trouble. Her tone of voice, way of walking, shoulder tilt, or eye level communicate almost instantly. Sometimes it takes a few minutes or two sentences, but usually not.

We also know there is a fire. The alarm has rung. We have the equipment, the concern, the experience, the dedication required to help. The problem is we can't find the flame.

Every spouse needs to get good at explaining the location of the blaze: "The flames are right over here. I have the fire under control; just give me some space"; or, "The flames are raging; I could use some help."

Partners are more than firefighters. We serve each other well by practicing fire prevention. When we need help in a hurry, though, spouses can hustle to the rescue.

Flexercise

1. What do you find is the hardest thing to share with your spouse? How might you make it easier?

2. How do you come to your spouse's aid when he crashes?

3. When you are depleted and deflated, how do you get this across to your family? Could you find a better way?

No More Pretending

I F ALL THE WORLD IS a stage and all the men and
women merely actors, where do we go to remove the
make-up? Life is more than a call to hide behind a
mask. Office administrators, policemen, teachers, ministers, doctors and secretaries are some of the people who
try to maintain their images rather than be themselves.

If a person can't find the freedom and safety at home
to abandon his script, take off his costume and forget about
his role, he or she can become a meteorite burning to ashes
in a friction-packed life.

Our Anxiety Level

The distance between who we are and who we pretend
to be is called our anxiety level. If our anxiety level is high,
we tend to put up a front each day, afraid people will discover who we really are. That's a great amount of pressure.
It's bad enough that we wear the mask every day, but the
discomfort becomes unbearable if we must wear that mask
everywhere.

Conservationists recognize the principle and provide
wildlife sanctuaries. Animals can be aggravated, trapped
and shot all over the country. But if they are to survive as
a species, they must have safety zones where they can feed,
rest, procreate and revive themselves.

Our home needs to serve as a human sanctuary where
we can take time out, be ourselves and feel accepted. Because we have safety zones, we are better able to charge

back out and wrestle the world on its own terms.

One of the major pleasures of being married is getting to know another person well. This is a large part of what makes a marriage work. Each of us is more amazing than the Grand Canyon or a TransAm engine. Frequently we hear someone say, "After fifteen years Jack and I have gotten to know each other really well."

Unfortunately, too many couples spend too many of their years merely breaking the surface. If partners are to last, they must cut through the pretension and get to know each other more rapidly.

Mask Removal

When we talk about removing our masks, at least two major fears rush to the surface;

1. We fear this is an invitation to immediately become rude and obnoxious.

Rudeness is never acceptable and it ought to be a legitimate concern. If we are mean and thoughtless beneath our masks, then we definitely have something we need to work on. The problem will not be erased by keeping it hidden.

Let our spouse help us one layer at a time as we let the mask slip off and we handle rudeness together.

2. We worry that neither our partner nor ourselves will like what is beneath the mask.

Mask removing is risky business but it is far less dangerous than keeping it in place. As we move toward a less pretentious and less fearful self, we will find the real us far more likeable than the uptight, shifty, deceitful us. You can count on it.

Our old friend Paul was able to express his openness this way: "You know we never used flattery, nor did we put on a mask to cover up greed—God is our witness." (1 Thessalonians 2:5).

Each of us will like the real self better than the phony one.

Transparency

Smart couples move toward transparency. Our partner should be able to see through us. We invite him to know how we act, dream, think, lust, fear, hope.

My wife knows how I lust. That wasn't an easy hurdle to overcome, but it has been liberating. Pat has no strange feeling that some murky evil is going on in my mind that she knows nothing about. No terrible temptation waits to break out of the corral and run wild. The fact that she understands helps tame the beast and make it more manageable.

She and I don't spend our days and nights hoping the other one never finds out what we are like. The more we understand, both weak and strong, the more we appreciate each other. We haven't reached a plateau where we talk about everything, but we are closer now than we ever have been before.

The more light shining on our lives, the more we are able to change ourselves and appreciate who we actually are. Ecclesiastes 2:13 states the principle: "I saw that wisdom is better than folly, just as light is better than darkness."

Tearing Off Masks

Removing our own mask is one operation. Tearing the mask off our partner is altogether another. Never force a person to reveal what he is not ready to disclose. It's a violation of our integrity to have anyone pull out our feelings if we are unwilling. The results could be so agonizing as to chase the individual back into a shell and make it much harder for him to emerge later.

A simple, "I don't feel comfortable talking about it now," should be a sufficient warning to any sensitive partner. We do not force openness. We create a safe atmosphere where openness is more likely to occur naturally.

Ken explained how he unknowingly destroyed all self expression in his marriage. "I wanted to make us the open couple where it all hung out. If Lois sneezed, I wanted to know what that meant and I wanted to know now. I'd sit her down on the couch practically every day and insist she spill her guts. It was more like an inquisition than openness. I drove her nuts."

A person's openness must be free to stay closed until that person is ready to be open.

Childlike

Don't be surprised if by dropping our guard we slightly regress when at home. Most of us tire of pretending. We are adult, and feel we must be totally under control, aggressive and cool when in public. As one observer has said, our home may appear to be our castle, but inside, it is more like a nursery.

Accept a certain amount of retreating, a great deal of playfulness and a bit of childlikeness as our partners unravel. They not only tend to become who they really are but also who they might like to be.

This need not be frightening. Be thankful for the spouse who can become like a child. He tends to live longer, is more creative and, if it is done in balance, he is much more fun to live with.

Think about King David who lived under tremendous pressure and uncertainty. On two particularly notable occasions, he took time to let off steam. On one occasion he went after another man's wife and had the husband killed. A second time David relaxed by leaping and dancing in the streets as if he were seven years old (2 Samuel 6:16). If given the choice, we know which form of release we would want our spouse to use.

There is a movie in which Jack Nicholson and Meryl Streep are married. One evening they order a pizza and just the two of them eat, giggle, sing, joke and enjoy each other. They are two great actors and you can see love, happiness and fun dancing in their eyes. In those few minutes you see them let their defenses down while they become small children daring to laugh about nothing and to drink in the fullness of the moment.

Every marriage partner should have the freedom to let go and be himself.

Flexercise

1. What is the most childlike thing you like to do? When did you last do it?

2. How would you describe your transparency level with your spouse?

3. Who do you think have the most trouble removing masks, men or women? Explain.

Giving In

S AM AND TERRI MARRIED in their early thirties,
and it was the first time for both. Prior to their marriage, each had arranged his life in almost meticulous
order. Each knew where his tennis racket hung, his tea bags
were stashed and his shorts stacked. Each knew there was
one place to put shoes. Each was certain how the toilet
paper had to come off the roll.

There is nothing wrong with being orderly. Would that
we all practiced neatness. But Sam and Terri were not just
orderly; they worshipped the order they had acquired. Because they had lived contentedly independent for ten years,
they weren't about to look for new ways to stack shelves or
squeeze toothpaste tubes.

All of us come to marriage with a territorial sense.
That can be healthy to a point. If you need a quiet time in
the morning or evening, space to meditate or pull your soul
together, your partner needs to respect that. And you're
not to bully your way into every corner of your mate's life.
With an attitude called respect, we honor the personal
traits of our spouse, the breathing room, the quirks, the od-
dities.

That, however, was not Sam and Terri's approach.
They had forgotten what flexibility was — they hadn't practiced it in years. Neither had argued over which television
show to watch. They cooked what they ate and ate what
they cooked. They went to bed when they felt like it, and
got up when they had to.

Sam and Terri married with a reasonable amount of fear. Both expected they would have to change. Unfortunately, neither knew how much give and take would be required. In the first two weeks each began to claim his own territory. After six months they realized there was little they were willing to rearrange. By their first anniversary, they were keeping court dates with men who carried dark briefcases.

Types of Marriage Relationship

We can see several different types of marriage relationships if we observe enough couples. The following list will help give us a handle on some of those types. Try to decide which *best* describes your relationship.

HE . . . SHE	**Territorial**—Each lives independently under the same roof.
HE SHE	**Stratified**—This is a boss/servant relationship.
HE SHE	**Benevolent dictator**—He doesn't give many orders but when he does she'd better jump.
sH^E H_E	**Unstructured**—Neither partner knows where their relationship stands. Each approaches it with fear and uncertainty.
HE/SHE	**Mutual respect**—Each spouse gives and takes with reasonable ease. They try to reach decisions together. Compromise is not a dirty word but a pleasure.

Unfortunately, Sam and Terri's territorial sense hardened to the point where their relationship fit too well under the "territorial" heading above. Territorial marriages almost never work. Occasionally, couples do live together in independence, but not often. Usually each is saying, "I can do anything I want and you can do anything I want." And they call it independence. Actually, he claims his space, hobbies, time zones, sleeping habits, and she stakes out hers. They tend to live separately and mix with each other only when it doesn't violate their priorities.

If either one takes a servant role, the marriage is not truly territorial but stratified. That is, they believe their roles are rigidly defined and divinely appointed. He doesn't cook; she doesn't get the oil changed. He watches ball games; she dusts. When in doubt over their roles, he decides who does what.

Neither of these types of marriage is based on love, equality or friendship.

In a benevolent dictator type marriage, at his core the man feels superior but is proud of the fact that he doesn't push his wife around. However, when he needs to reach back and marshal his authority, he reluctantly does so. In some cases she is the Benevolent Dictator, holding her force in reserve only because she believes it is "unladylike" to show her power.

Mutual Respect

We have seen examples of practically any type of marriage work. They may not be happy or fulfilled, but the couple stays together with a reasonable amount of congeniality. However, the marriages that seem to work best for most people are founded on mutual respect, cooperation, sharing and love which promote great inter-personal relationships.

Compromise

The word *compromise* has a bad reputation. Too many of us believe we know what is right and we must follow it. That may be true in morals, sports and theology, but marriage is more fluid and adjustable. Here compromise takes on a dignity worthy of poets, noblemen and lovers.

The dictionary tells me that to compromise is to adjust or settle by mutual concessions. That sounds like a marriage that could grow for fifty years.

Giving Love

Jesus Christ gave us a principle for life that works particularly well for marriage. He said it was more blessed to give than to receive (Acts 20:35). This ancient proverb makes us stand on our toes and become alert. Our first question is: How can I make him or her happy? The goal is not to gratify ourselves but to bring satisfaction to our partner.

Paul says in 1 Corinthians 13 that love is not self-seeking. We love someone; therefore, we try to serve him. Our perverted concept of love says we are in it for what we can get. Do we want sex, money, service, attention, nursing, protection, security and partnership? Then we should get married. Well, if we make those our goals, we distort the foundations of marriage. We marry to give to the person we love. Almost automatically we receive love in return.

Unfortunately, we have manipulated marriage to the place where women are perceived as the giving, sharing, helping, nurturing partners. The male is often seen as little King Tut who gets his boots chewed, whoopee cushion puffed and brow mopped.

Getting the Picture

Smart couples realize that the Christian concept of love is higher than mere role playing. The major goal of a married person is to please his or her spouse. Read that sentence again.

Then take the brief survey on the next page. How do you contribute to your marriage? (1 is the pits; 10 is highest) Try to be fair. Don't ask how much your partner gives, but for now search only your own heart.

MARRIAGE CONTRIBUTION SURVEY

Emotionally	1 2 3 4 5 6 7 8 9 10	
Financially	1 2 3 4 5 6 7 8 9 10	
Physically (household)	1 2 3 4 5 6 7 8 9 10	
Sexually	1 2 3 4 5 6 7 8 9 10	
Conversationally	1 2 3 4 5 6 7 8 9 10	
Spiritually	1 2 3 4 5 6 7 8 9 10	
Goal setting	1 2 3 4 5 6 7 8 9 10	
Eat leftovers	1 2 3 4 5 6 7 8 9 10	
Handle TV control	1 2 3 4 5 6 7 8 9 10	

So how do you like what you see? How much are you really giving to your relationship?

Nonmanipulative

Giving that calculates, maneuvers and exploits does not qualify as love-giving. Since we possess few pure motives, we all probably give to get to some extent. Sometimes we give good sex to get good sex. That isn't earth-shaking, evil or cruel. But when *most of our actions* are devious and self-serving, we put our relationship at risk.

A near fatal mistake we make is to picture marriage as a "deal" that will bring us gigantic dividends. It's a fallacy believed by both males and females. Marriage must first be an avenue to *express* our love.

Gary told me, "I got married to get what I could. Who was going to feed me? Who was going to love me? Who was going to wash my clothes, vacuum, fix the drapes? I knew I couldn't get along without a wife. I never thought about what I would give her. I imagined she would be happy just to have me around."

When a marriage is primarily a place to reap love

rather than plant it, the relationship will experience enormous stress.

Satisfied couples lean more and more toward pleasing each other. They see their partners more as an object of their affection and less as simply an object.

You and I are filled with love. We have it by nature and we have gained even more through Christ. Smart people look for good outlets to pour out that love. That principle is sound. (It becomes an outrageous concept, though, when one person rejects it. If the wife is giving, giving, giving, and her husband is taking, taking, taking, this foundation block becomes a sandhill.)

Don't brush this precept off easily. The main reason marriages burn out is that we fail to see partnership as a giving relationship.

The Place of Sacrifice

Nebuchadnezzar, the king of Babylon, married a woman from a far-off hilly country. When he saw how miserable she was in his flat land, the king weighed his options. He could live in an estranged relationship for the next forty years or he might find a way to make his wife happy. His response was to build the Hanging Gardens of Babylon, one of the Seven Wonders of the World. You and I could probably amaze our spouses with only half the extravagance.

The problem is we tend to exaggerate our amount of sacrifice. We worry that we are giving in too often. At the same time we are suspicious that we shouldn't give in at all. This is the generation that believes you can have everything. Many are not prepared to wait, or to suspend or lower their desire for gratification. That attitude produces a terrible drag on any relationship.

A certain segment of society feels that marriage should not cost us, that child-bearing should not cost us, that relationships should not carry a price tag. Yet cost is a normal and honorable process. A car costs money; a friend costs time. A painted house costs energy; a relationship costs intimacy. A waxed floor costs elbow grease; understanding costs risk and openness.

Happy couples learn to sacrifice gladly.

Flexercise

1. Surprise your spouse tonight. Do something that will make him or her happy — no strings attached.

2. How would you describe your marriage relationship (i.e., territorial, mutual, etc.)? Explain.

3. Who is the most giving in your relationship? Why do you say that?

Commitment Is Back In Style

C OMMITMENT SOUNDS GRIM. We would like to think people stay married for higher reasons. Passion, love, purpose, meaning, happiness, children, all have a cheerful ring to them. Commitment is more like a concrete block. Steady, dependable—and dull.

For a while I used to think it was the worst reason in the world to remain married, but through the years I've become more and more aware of the gift of simple commitment. Some days marriage doesn't seem to make sense. No passion that day. We can't find a spark. Everything seems dark and dreary in our relationship. That's the day or weekend when you grab hold of that block called commitment and you ride out the storm.

By Monday the passions start to flow again. You are patting each other in the kitchen. You get out the map and begin planning a one-day trip to see the prairie dogs.

What would have happened if we had a low opinion of commitment? Every storm, even every low tide would become a threat to our marriage.

Feelings That Come and Go

Feelings are tremendously important to a married couple. Too often we have treated feelings with contempt. But the philosophy that says, "If the feeling isn't there, get out," fails to understand the flow and temperament of feelings. It fails to comprehend how feelings can be created, developed and improved. Feelings need to be kept at a healthy level, but we can't afford to jump ship just because our feelings have run aground.

When our feelings were high, but unfortunately negative, my wife squared off, looked me in the eye and said, "Hey, I'm not easy to get rid of. I'm going to work at this and turn it around."

Pat declared her commitment. That gave both of us hope while we worked on our feelings.

Marriage Vows

It seems popular to ridicule marriage vows, and some enter and leave marriage like they do a revolving door. The vows probably need to be revised; ideally a couple should write their own. However they are presented, though, marriage vows serve a valid purpose. The couple knows they have promised faithfulness and commitment. They have promised God and themselves that they will make their marriage work, hopefully in a delightful and glad fashion.

What could be wrong with that?

The purpose of marriage vows is not to bond to sour dispositions for the next forty years. By making a pledge, the couple agrees to give the relationship vitality, not merely lumber through it.

Testing the Waters

How can a couple make a commitment when they know each other so little before they get married? That is a tough problem and always will be. We do marry strangers. Part of the solution is to be sure you are marrying a good stranger. Thoughtfulness, integrity, faith, generosity and communication are basic planks that help solid people build solid marriages.

Experimental marriage is a bad idea. The concept of

trying marriage as one would conduct studies in a science laboratory has a history of poor results. We want to think living together will be a good learning ground, but normally our glands control our brain cells.

The concept of a "non-committal commitment" defies all logic and we know it. It's like practicing to be Irish. You either are or you aren't. We can't live together and pretend we are committed to see if we like being committed.

When our marriage begins to rock, we wonder how we got into this mess. Should we have lived together and maybe have discovered that we were not meant for each other?

Several studies indicate the folly of "practice" marriages. One, a study of Swedish women who lived with their men before marriage, has shown disastrous results. The couples who had lived together had an 80 percent higher divorce rate than those who had not.

This does not demonstrate that living together caused the divorces. Rather, these women may never have been committed to the idea of marriage. However, it does show that living together failed to make these women better able to accept the commitment of marriage.

If you had lived together you probably would not have been one iota better prepared for marriage. Read that sentence again.

Living together has grown much more popular in the United States, yet at this writing only four percent of couples choose this route. The numbers of those who have lost their virginity are much higher, but living together is not flooding the nation.

Don't envy the carefree couples who live together without benefit of clergy. Those relationships do not work as well as some would have us believe. Find the strength and goodness in the decision you made. Looking over your shoulder at mythical options will only hinder you from making the most of now.

Shallow Concept

Recently a movie star and her equally famous fiancé announced their engagement. Despite previous difficulties with their relationships, they expressed confidence that this marriage would be different. As a token of their undying fidelity each had a tattoo of the other's name engraved on his or her rear. What more could any couple do to "pledge their troth"?

Unfortunately, they never made it to the altar, and now have canceled their engagement. Apparently even branding is not enough to guarantee a lasting partnership if there is no commitment.

Since our society is marked by instability and mobility, commitment frequently comes across as entrapment. We change jobs often. We spend thousands of dollars to get a college education then take the same job we could have had the day we walked out of high school. The emphasis on doing our own thing, exercising total freedom, and walking out on our problems, is appealing. Even the housing we choose is often temporary or transitory as if we don't want to get tied down.

If trends dictate our lives, we feel that styles change so quickly we need to hang loose. Hanging loose sounds like a weak foundation for a marriage.

The Basic Principle

There are no easy formulas for a successful marriage. Each of us must work out our relationship in the best way we are able to. Because relationships are fragile and tricky, we should not stop to judge other couples on the decisions they make.

That doesn't mean we have no principles to hold on to. Jesus Christ expressed the main rule as this: "Therefore what God has joined together, let man not separate" (Matthew 19:6).

God, well aware of the chaos created when people jump

from marriage to marriage, wants every couple to adjust and grow, and to find fulfillment in each other.

He looks for couples to make the sacrifices necessary to blend into a happy partnership, not because we have to, but because we want to. After all, isn't that why we got married, because we wanted to?

A Buffer

Some fear that commitment will lead to taking each other for granted. It could—but it doesn't have to. Commitment says, "I forgot to call and say I'd be late, but I will apologize, and I will make up for it." Commitment also says, "I know he will not blow up, pack and head out. He will remain long enough for us to work this out."

Flexercise

1. Do you remember a time when you sat tight and let the marital storm blow over? What was it like?

2. How deeply do you feel committed to your marriage?

3. How have you seen your marriage grow in commitment?

Our Duty Is Self Care

B ILL JUST KIND OF CRAWLS home every evening. He reads the paper, eats supper and parks himself in front of the TV. He never has any energy left over for me," his wife Margie complained. "I don't expect him to go sky diving, but how about a walk in the park, or maybe he could push the cart at the supermarket? I'd have to dress like a Chicago Bear linebacker just to get him to look at me."

Imagine being married to someone who seldom feels good. He isn't "up" to going out, or working in the yard, or having friends over. Always drained, he holds you down from doing what you might enjoy.

That picture sounds dismal. Now, compound the scenario by realizing that your spouse is that way out of simple neglect. He doesn't have enough spunk even to try to keep up, and thereby creates a serious drain on the relationship.

Discovering What Changed

Bill may have shown signs of stagnation while he and Margie were dating but his immobility probably wasn't this severe. If he changed drastically after marriage, he needs to find the switch that turned him off.

He may have had an attitude change that has turned into a physical malfunction. Is he disillusioned about himself or his marriage? He could be in the wrong job. He could be on the wrong diet. Maybe he suffers from a low grade illness. Possibly he simply doesn't care. Whatever the reason, right now he's living the life of an anemic slug.

As an act of love Bill needs to find a way to improve his health and energy level. He may not be able to pull himself out without someone to talk to. The sooner he can air out his feelings with a friend, counselor or minister, the sooner he can attack his lethargy.

Modest Improvements

We all know people like Bill, and we also know people who need a radical and immediate change in their lifestyles, a major program to rescue their physical fitness. That's not true of most of us, though, which is good since that sort of thing intimidates so many of us. But if you're a little bit like Bill, don't hesitate to try something just because you can't or won't go for the big program. Actually three or four small alterations may be all you need.

How about a short walk over terrain with a noticeable upgrade, just enough to make the ticker speed up a tad? What would you think of switching a glass of soft drink or a cup of coffee with a glass of water during the evening? How about ten push-ups in the morning? That little bit of change in routine could improve the way you act and think.

Our goal is two-pronged: (1) We want to be more alive today, with more spunk for our marriage and for life in general; and (2) we want to live longer—we owe it to our spouse to live as long as we can, and to be as well as we can. We betray the trust he put in us and we bruise the love we share by fooling around with our health.

This in no way reflects on people who cannot help their illness or handicap. Actually, people in wheelchairs, diabetics, or cancer patients often make great marriage partners. Both partners should evaluate the situation, provide for limitations, and make the most of all their benefits.

Protecting Our Minds

In addition to respecting our bodies, as much as is in our power we need to protect our minds. We owe it to the ones we love.

Often we act as though mental health were a lost cause. We seem to believe you either have mental health or you don't. All of us have mental glitches from time to time, though. We might be low on sugar, high on sugar, overloaded on adrenaline or saturated with coffee. These things can affect the way we think, especially in the short term.

We also might be cantankerous simply because we "feel like" being mean. Each of us has that capability.

We run the chance of serious burnout if we play too many mind games with ourselves and our mate. If we intentionally use depression to escape responsibility, we torture our partner. If we depend on negativism to avoid trying anything new, we keep our spouse on the ropes. When we use self-pity as a cop-out so we don't have to stand up and be counted, we leave our mate with a sponge when he needs a rock. Anyone who chooses to run a sloppy mind makes a miserable mess of marriage.

For example, one young mother told me, "Joe is always playing mind games with us. We're all afraid to talk to him. If we say anything, he is liable to jump either left or right. He might collapse into a blue funk, or he could lift off into euphoria. Some days he's all right but other times it's like the San Diego Zoo around here."

We need to watch for those kinds of "fits" and control them before we become self-indulgent and abusive.

The destructive mental patterns we develop are big, ugly criminals. Some people use anger as a regular method of manipulation. Some spouses sulk to get their way. These people have nurtured harmful mental patterns and are using them to scramble their mates psychologically.

Many of us have come from families where sloppy thinking and demoralizing mental habits were a way of life.

Changing long-time patterns is asking a great deal, but it isn't impossible. We often meet people who think far differently today from the way they used to think.

This does not suggest that some of us may be faking mental problems. Many people suffer genuine mental and psychological difficulties, but those who can must try to improve their mental outlook. It's a necessary act of love. The fact is, there are a number of measures we can take to protect our minds.

The solution to our mental attitude may be medical help, counseling, self-improvement or painful self-correction. We do others a great service by looking for ways to protect our minds. So go for it. When tempted to head for the ditch, grab hold of the wheel. Head back for the middle of the road.

Ultimate Risks

Without exaggerating the risks involved, we have to consider people who put more at stake than just their energy level. Some of us risk early disability or even death with too little regard for the partner we will hurt.

Lori told me, "If I stop to think about it, I really resent what Gary did. He liked to race cars and take big chances. Then he had that terrible accident and now he's gone, and I have two children to raise alone. I get angry at the cars sometimes — and at Gary."

If he had stopped smoking . . . if she had controlled her blood pressure . . . if he had exercised . . . Phrases like these bounce around in many people's minds, often without being said, but these people do harbor serious resentments.

We would consider any person reckless if he failed to provide for his family in case of his early death. The same foolishness prevails if we rattle around not half caring how our actions might affect the people we love. Many of us knowingly fool with our health. We eat things that we know will wreck our stomachs. We ignore the first signs of illness.

We take ridiculous risks in sports or horseplay. And we do it as if we don't care how it affects anyone. In fact, some spouses purposely play roulette with their health to get attention. Gambling like that is immature and maddening.

I'd be cruel if I asked my partner to be married to someone who intentionally risks his health (me). Love does not knowingly taunt its partner by making him worry. Love aims to provide, protect and care for the object of that love. We owe it to each other not to take unreasonable chances.

A Special Gift

For the special gift that fits all sizes, give your spouse a bona fide, healthy you. As far as possible, be a fine-tuned, efficient, 100,000-mile model that your mate will thoroughly appreciate.

That doesn't mean we have to run the twenty-six-mile marathon, eat acorns, or hop around the living room with Richard Simmons. Extreme fitness isn't the issue here. As an act of love, we can reduce the anxiety our spouses go through. We can also diminish the amount of "down time" we suffer from unnecessary illness simply by taking reasonable care of our bodies.

We can also reduce the amount of spiritual "down time" by exercising some focused care.

Spiritual Health

Spirituality has its own rewards. The benefits of keeping in touch with Jesus Christ are immediate. The help given by the Holy Spirit is personal and enriching.

Out of that deep well of resource flows an added strength to nourish our marriage. Constant contact with Christ gives us a set of values and an outlook on life which supplies instant rewards to our relationship.

Read again the description of the fruit of the Spirit in Galatians 5:22,23. Each ingredient of that fruit is ripe for the marriage experience. Love, joy, peace, patience, kindness, goodness, faithfulness, gentleness and self-control foster a long-term, robust partnership.

When you aim for your own spiritual fulfillment, the bull's eye you hit will encompass a marriage that can become strong and vibrant.

A proverb says: "Do not be wise in your own eyes; fear the LORD and shun evil. This will bring health to your body and nourishment to your bones" (3:7,8).

Not to mention what it will do for your love life.

Flexercise

---

1. How can you help your body help your marriage?

2. What mental pattern would you like to improve? How could you go about it?

3. How would you describe your spiritual life? How does it affect your marriage? Is there something about it you would like to change?

Sex as Quality Fuel

WHEN WE FIRST GOT MARRIED, we imagined that hot sex would last forever. Except for a few setbacks, a couple of misunderstandings and possibly an adjustment or two, the wild passion continued. And it was a blast. There may not have been a great deal of lovemaking, but the physical satisfaction rode high.

Since life moves forward for most people, and jobs must be maintained, sex activity might slow a pace or two. Other priorities rush in and we begin to reach a balance. Unfortunately for too many of us, sex doesn't level off but continues to slide until it reaches a dangerously low end of the scale.

Burnout is more likely among couples:

● who have no sex;

● who have little sex;

● who argue continuously over sex;

● where one person receives almost no satisfaction.

Few couples who give up sex or almost never have it still get along swimmingly.

Benefits of Sex

Sex serves a function, which goes beyond procreation. Sex:

1. "Feeds" the skin
2. Communicates love

3. Builds security
4. Provides fun and excitement
5. Enhances self-esteem
6. Fights temptation
7. Cuts the tension
8. Eliminates the need to play checkers

Though not the only source for these qualities, sex is a major tributary. Without sex, many other sources must be tapped to take its place.

A few couples can survive without meaningful sex; however, most marriages will suffer because of the drain the lack of sex places on other areas. That drain may overload our resources and result in burnout.

Contrary to the view that sex is merely a hedonistic practice aimed at base pursuits, it actually plays a significant role in marriage most of us cannot afford to forfeit.

Michelle described the situation quite clearly when she said, "If we go a week without sex, we can really tell. Our nerves seem frazzled and we're irritable. After lying together, making love and being cuddly, our relationship improves immediately."

Most couples I have listened to express their feelings in a similar way.

It may be possible to have a gratifying sex life and still not get along—but it's improbable. Sex is too intimate, too fulfilling in a marriage to allow for much hostility. Some have regular sex and don't care for each other, but I know from experience: It's tricky to maintain antagonistic sex.

But since there is so much immorality, each man should have his own wife, and each woman her own husband. The husband should fulfill his marital duty to his wife, and likewise the wife to her husband. The wife's body does not belong to her alone but also to her husband. In the same way, the husband's body does not belong to him alone but also to his wife. Do

after the fireworks. They feel more secure, more appreciated and totally loved.

Extra Steps to Sensational Sex

1. *Study your partner's body*

Find his (or her) favorite weakness and drive him crazy. You probably won't discover it during the first few months or year of marriage, but you don't need it then. General sex leaves most of us half-blind during those exploratory days anyway.

Everybody has a button or two. When you find the mystery areas, play them like Mozart. Later the areas may change. Then hunt for the new ones.

2. *Have a game plan*

Set aside enough time, energy and space to play bedroom games. Begin to think ahead of what you might like to do before you go to your room.

Get your mind in gear. Whisper what you are thinking. If it's half-civil, your partner may start turning to jelly.

3. *Get exotic*

The day of always needing darkness has passed. Romantic music, special clothes, scented candles — that's how Solomon would have done it. A bath, a spot of perfume and a bowl of grapes. Go for it.

4. *Sex holidays*

Daily love is great but those special trips are mind boggling. Why not go away for a day, a weekend, a week for the main purpose of having sex? Don't let some ancient taboo make you feel guilty. Couples go on holidays to play golf or tennis or to go shopping. Why not a lovemaking vacation?

Besides terrific tonics for today, love holidays make amazing memories. And memories provide great fuel for the days ahead.

Why do we talk so much about sex? Because it plays a

large role in the lives of most married couples. Done incorrectly, sex results in bitterness; but when taken at its best, sex becomes a super source of high-premium petroleum.

Flexercise

1. If you ignore sex, how many days does it take to affect your relationship? How can you tell?

2. Do you ever feel "skin-starved"? If so, what do you do about it?

3. If you could pick any location to go to—to make love—where would you go?

Oiling Your Squeaks

F OR AROUND A DOLLAR we can buy a small can of oil and keep most of our equipment in fairly good condition. A few squirts on the door hinges, a quick shot behind the fan, a couple of drops in an engine, and it's amazing how long things continue to run.

Transfer that image to our marriage. If each of us accepts the position of "oil-can controller," our unions will last longer and run more smoothly. Maybe oil-can controller sounds like too piddling a job for some of us, but it beats the thunder out of a major breakdown.

Our job description is twofold. **First**, it is preventive maintenance. That means we squirt before things squeak. **Second,** it assures quick repair. We catch minor squeaks before they cause major damage; we squirt before they drive anyone crazy.

Everyone understands these simple terms. They apply to human dynamics as well as to primitive machines. If we forget to oil our relationships, we will wear them away.

Why We Don't Oil

Normally we neglect the job of oiling for two reasons. **First,** we think the other person is responsible ("I'm not going to keep working at this if he isn't"). **Second,** we don't know where or how to oil. ("I can never figure out what she wants.")

We have to resolve these two problems. For starters, every married person has to assume the role of "head of oil

99

can control." None of us can wait for or expect the other person to do it. That would result in a stalemate between two persons who are too foolish and too stubborn to move.

Getting the Job Done

Another reason *you* must take this job in hand is that no one can oil-can like you can. Don't get bigheaded—it isn't the kind of thing you include in your resumé—but this is a fact: What your spouse needs oiled, she needs you to oil!

If you accept that position, your marriage will run like grandfather's clock.

Okay, you've taken the job. Now, how do you carry it out? Half the time it seems like we squirt oil behind the refrigerator when it's the air conditioner that is shooting out the blue smoke.

Whether your spouse is male or female, you can't go wrong by keeping the oil flowing in these three areas:

1. Thoughtfulness.

All of us want to be thought of and thought of well. Any evidence we give to indicate our spouse is at the top of our thinking will be hugely appreciated. Phone calls, notes and small gifts are not lost on the person we love. Any clue that a wife is as important as the Dallas Cowboys is bound to make her happier. Thoughtfulness knows no gender gap. Both sexes want to be remembered with joy.

2. Helpfulness.

Whether it's washing dishes or replacing spark plugs, each of us notices any extra help we get. Anything that will lighten the load, even in a symbolic sense, makes a spouse feel terrific. Each person may have separate responsibilities but helpfulness crosses all lines.

3. Mindfulness of Value.

Every spouse needs to feel like a million bucks plus

change. The fact that you want to be near him or her, touching, talking, listening and sharing helps build that sense of value. Each time we oil someone's self-worth, we speed up our engine of solid relationship.

Eric is the kind of husband who should be teaching marriage seminars. He's a great oil-can man. On almost any day you can see Eric running around with his can going pop-pop. He squirts a shot here, a double shot there.

As a thoughtful person, he tries to look ahead. He knows his wife, Lori, has to work late Wednesday night so he thinks it through. When Lori gets home around 10:15, he will have a plate of crackers and a glass of milk waiting. He will lay out her nightclothes and pull the bedspread back. If he has any mints, he will put one on her pillow a la Hotel Hotshot.

None of that will change Lori's life materially, but what a sparkle it will bring to her spirit. It costs Eric ten minutes work and a pinch of forethought. In return he gets a well-tuned relationship and a wife who thinks he's Prince Hunk. Pop-pop. Pop-pop.

Eric has no special gifts or insight into human nature. Anyone can do what he does.

The Nurturing Role

Putting people into categories creates false distinctions. For instance, we assign women to the imaginary role of nurturing: Only females can hold, comfort, heal and nurse.

With that conclusion, men tend to concede the role and shy away from helping. No wonder we see so few Erics. But God created men to nurture as well as women. To maintain a balanced relationship men must reclaim part of that role.

"He doesn't want to know. [I'll never forget the frustration on Sonja's face.] He can't even find the children's pajamas. He doesn't know where the mixing spoon is. He doesn't know where the children keep their toys. And he isn't about to find out! He thinks all of this is outside his duties. Well, the children belong to him, too."

A wife cannot be the only nurturer in the family. If she were, who would nurture her?

Oiling What's Been Neglected

Look back for a moment at areas that have been too long ignored and forgotten. Critical parts of your relationship may be about to freeze up. If so, head for the oil can before it's too late.

Maybe you have given up intimacy or talking or prime time together. Possibly trips are important and you haven't taken one for years. Have you failed to keep a promise you made long ago? Keeping a forgotten promise is better than money from the government.

Take a good look; then go to work.

The Oil of Joy

In Bible times olive oil was the remedy for almost everything. Folks poured it on their food, drank it as medicine, rubbed down each other's backs, slicked down their hair, and used the oil as a deodorant. The Jews washed feet, anointed priests, softened skin, filled their lamps, bathed the dead — all with olive oil.

Olive groves covered the countryside as a booming agricultural industry. People moved daily on the lubricant of olive oil.

Every Jew understood Psalm 45:7. The author wrote that God anoints us with the oil of joy. Joy has the same effect as oil. Joy lifts the spirit, enriches the body and perks up the relationship.

Joy is a contagious attitude. Fragrant with hope, optimism, fulfillment and anticipation, joy actually can infect everyone in our home.

A smart partner will take charge of the department of joy. "It's my role to speak of good things. It's my job to find the positive side of meatloaf. It's my responsibility to paint an evening at home as a treat with many treasures to explore. It's my goal to unearth some pleasure out of a trip to the mall."

You are the General of Joy. None of us can afford to leave that to someone else. We shrivel up waiting for others to take the initiative and make joy happen. "Anointing with the oil of joy is my job."

Flexercise

1. What long-standing area of your life would you like to have oiled? Have you told your partner?

2. How do you picture your performance as an oil-can person? Are you doing a good job?

3. Name one area in which you could do a better job of oiling.

Spiritual Meaning

HOW DO YOU KNOW your marriage will be interesting? What guarantee do you have against a boring relationship? How many boats will it take, how many trips to Europe, how many racing cars before you get a kick out of living together?

All of these events and possessions can be fun. We have had our share. But in order for a couple to reach lasting satisfaction they need something more significant than fun. They need to reach out for meaning. To discover meaning we must find a spiritual plane.

Don't let "spiritual plane" frighten you. We aren't talking about nights in the desert eating grubs nor are we suggesting some sort of soul barbecuing. We're talking about a higher, more purposeful level of living.

What do we mean? **First,** we recognize that people do not live by bread alone. Clothes, cars, travelogues, concerts, and homes do not form the essence of life. Couples totally wrapped up in their own desires and goals normally find life tasteless and dull, but there exists a spiritual dimension that in the final analysis causes life to make sense. Seeking and reaching this spiritual dimension together will provide the longest burning, and most effective fuel for your marriage.

Second, we acknowledge that many ways exist to help others and serve God which bring a sense of satisfaction and meaning, including teaching children, caring for the

elderly, helping prisoners, and furnishing food for the be-
reaved. Practically any service by which we reach outside
ourselves gives us spiritual meaning.

Third, we can find this spiritual meaning in Jesus
Christ. When we invite Him into our lives, God's Holy
Spirit takes up residence inside us and begins to monitor
our spiritual lives. The Holy Spirit makes us spiritually sensitive and opens our eyes to ways to reach out to others.

Nonchristians

Millions of nonchristian couples are learning these
same basic principles. Sports figures, executives, movie
stars and plumbers are all increasingly aware that life has
more to offer than the opportunity to grab, collect, hoard
and stash. Couples who live by bread alone tend to stall and
gag.

As the author of Ecclesiastes put it: "And I saw that
all labor and all achievement spring from man's envy of his
neighbor. This too is meaningless, a chasing after the wind"
(4:4).

In chasing to accumulate, many chase a wind they can
never catch.

On the other hand, musicians collect money to feed
the hungry. Movie stars march to protest war. Average
citizens go to jail taking a stand against abortion. Busi-
nessmen head drives to help the handicapped. They all do
these things because they see there is more to life than
living like selfish bores.

Wealthy families in West Palm Beach, Florida, or-
ganize charity balls, festivals and auctions to express another side of life. Possibly they could party day and night,
but in these acts of kindness they acknowledge that there
is more to life than partying.

Sometimes we stop to ridicule these "pagans" for their
attempts at kindness, but in reality they teach us a lesson.
All of us reach out for meaning. The fortunate ones find a

spiritual plane and tie into it.

Living Examples

The people who find meaning to life stick their necks out and rise above their own everyday needs and desires.

Meet Bob and Lillian. They had plenty to do in their family business, but they decided to reach out and help prisoners. Soon they were teaching seminars, writing letters, offering transportation, even inviting prisoners into their homes. They shared Christ with the young men and women they met and gave them hope. As a team they found a way to rise onto a spiritual plane. They could feel the satisfaction of fulfilling a mission beyond themselves.

When a Laotian family moved to their town, Cindy and Ed got their family involved in helping. Their children started teaching English to the new arrivals. They furnished clothing, food and transportation. They spent Sunday afternoons teaching the parents how to drive. The Laotians found jobs and quickly became self-supporting. The children entered school and some did exceedingly well. The Laotians allowed Cindy and Ed to stretch. The added dimension did not make their normal family problems go away but it did minimize them and put them into perspective.

Steve and Carla enjoyed working with the middle class young people at church. Before long, however, the group took on a new complexion. By an unexplained twist the poor, underprivileged and disadvantaged filled the room. Week after week they discussed the pains of poverty, abuse, self-esteem, grades, broken homes and despair. More rewarding than jobs or hobbies, the young people filled a significant role in Steve and Carla's lives and family.

If you ever stopped to look at a new car, a new home, or a new boat, and said, "There must be more to life than this," you were right.

People do not live by bread alone.

Individual Efforts

Millions of husbands and wives go off alone to find meaning. She teaches a class; he works with a men's group. These important activities help the individuals feel fulfilled, which in turn benefits the couple's relationship.

However, split efforts may not be as meaningful as joint endeavors. When both pull together in a spiritual direction, they usually find mutual fulfillment, and spiritual bonding results.

Finding meaning on a spiritual level is not a cure-all, though. You still have to pick up your underwear, brush your teeth and balance your checkbook. Neither does finding this meaning lessen the importance of your children or the need for a decent vacation.

But we are likely to find added purpose, a key which helps dramatically to make sense out of life. If a husband or wife seeks that key only as an individual, the relationship might be further splintered — another example of a good thing resulting in a poor outcome.

Peg and John decided to bring prisoners to their community to paint a house. Basically Peg's project, she set up the committee, made the contacts, organized the housing, did the bulk of the planning. John made himself available. Whenever she needed to muster up another warm body, he jumped in. While Peg in essence did her own "spiritual" thing, she included John. They could fight the battle together and feel the same satisfaction. Consequently, they did not feel any pain of further separation brought on by a good cause.

All There Is?

The rich and the poor give the same cry: "Is this all there is?" Does one day blend into another until we die? Read Ecclesiastes, because meaning is the theme of the book. In one passage the author states:

> So my heart began to despair over all my toilsome labor under the sun. For a man may do his work with

wisdom, knowledge and skill, and then he must leave all he owns to someone who has not worked for it. This too is meaningless and a great misfortune (2:20,21).

Spiritual Oneness

If couples develop similar spiritual values, their relationship likely will remain strong. Dissimilar values result in dysfunction from general wear and tear. These people tend to have different views of morality, faithfulness, dedication and goals. If one person sees the goal of life as contacting UFOs and the other believes we find meaning by inhaling fragrances, we can almost see the trouble coming.

Spiritual unity comes when each marriage partner lives in close contact with God through Jesus Christ. They have an identical base from which to build and grow. Without that mutual platform they will find little in common of a spiritual nature.

As Christians they may find their growth to be even or they might use different forms. Some couples read the Bible and pray together. That works best for them. Others read the Bible separately and come together to discuss it. Others read the Bible strictly on their own and seldom share what they experience.

That's fine! Whatever! Rigid rules cannot dictate how couples grow in the Word of God. The Holy Spirit uses a wide variety of disciplines and methods. Don't get hung up on the method. Too many Christians give up their spiritual growth because they can't match Martin Luther or St. Francis of Assissi. Find your own pace.

You might be surprised at the style and routine set by many of our spiritual leaders. It's not as uniform and stiff as we might suppose. Three specific examples of styles used are: Read together. Read apart and discuss. Read apart and not discuss.

As partners mature, they discover the pattern for spiritual development that works best for them. That development normally includes knowledge of the Scripture, a desire to follow Jesus Christ, and an awareness of God's Spirit working in us. That's for starters.

Variety of Meaning

Spiritual meaning manifests itself in a wide spectrum. For some it involves meeting the physical needs around them. They will tutor, visit the lonely and seriously ill, feed the hungry. Others will teach or win the nonchristian to Christ. Possibly they will dedicate themselves to a ministry of prayer. Many will participate in a combination of the above.

Any person who adds risks for Jesus Christ to his life will reduce the boredom factor substantially. Couples who seek meaning together add spiritual fiber to an already healthy relationship and will continue to reach higher planes in their Christian lives.

"Never be lacking in zeal, but keep your spiritual fervor" (Romans 12:11).

Flexercise

---

1. What would you like you and your partner to do together as a spiritual service?

2. Do you have a place where the two of you could serve in the church, where you might feel meaningful? What is it?

3. What do you do to keep yourself growing spiritually?

Rekindling Romance

WHEN BOB ARRIVED HOME from work, his wife was waiting for him. She looked at her husband, blue eyes bouncing, and said, "Honey, trust me."

Bob hardly mumbled a protest before Ruth turned him around and began tying his hands. Giving the rope one final tug, she marched him out the door to her waiting car.

Twenty minutes later they checked into a motel. Ruth had decked the room with flowers, and robes hung across the chairs. Cackling her most sinister laugh, she pushed her smiling husband onto the water bed.

In Norton, Ohio, a husband devised a coupon book and gave it to his wife. He took a small spiral notebook and hand-wrote ten or fifteen coupons, each containing a promise which she could redeem at her will.

One coupon read: "One evening for dinner out at a place of your choice."

Another promised: "One evening I will cancel anything on my schedule (softball game, committee meeting, whatever) when you cash in this coupon."

Perhaps others promised flowers or a movie, possibly even a weekend in Cleveland. I don't know exactly because when I asked to look through the book, she gave me a polite but firm no. My imagination tells me it would have been great reading.

Enemies of Romance

Marriage has no worse enemy than *boredom*. Some couples sink into a dull routine of just getting by, until their union experiences more drudgery than pleasure. Without spark, meaning, or hope, too many partners merely plow through each day.

For many couples it wasn't always that way. They used to eat pizza and laugh into the night. They spent hours feeding ducks, skipping stones across the lake, and running to the top of the hill.

Some couples have kept the spirit of romance alive by adding a bit of spice here, an ounce of surprise there, and a dash of humor on the side. Those who have abandoned the love affair of their marriage and settled only for the bare knuckles of daily living risk burnout from boredom.

Romance appears to have several other enemies as well, causing some people to steer clear of it.

First, we seem to have dedicated ourselves to being practical. It's hard to get ahead, and both partners feel they must work feverishly for them to have all they want.

Second, books, movies and television have given romance a bad name. Often the media has made romance seem seedy rather than helpful. Soap operas present life as a daily disaster — steady marriages seem to be considered too boring to televise. Books often add illicit affairs for no apparent reason. I read an autobiography by a famous historian whom I admire very much. In the middle of the book the author described a one-night affair he had had with a correspondent. It was an ugly, awkward scene that had no place in the volume, but I suppose the point was to prove what a cool guy he thought he was. We are bombarded with torrid and sleazy immorality.

Third, romance is considered a low level of relationship. When in graduate school, I often observed how low love had sunk. Occasionally we'd have a special banquet, and a harried husband would shout to his wife as they passed in the kitchen, "Be sure to pick up your flower after work." No surprise. No pampering. Too little time to be tender. Their hectic world had to keep rattling along.

None of these needs to be true. Certainly a couple needs more than romance to keep their love alive. Ideally, all of us would have a multi-faceted relationship that includes spiritual values and good goals. But by forgetting the romance, we take the tingle out of marriage.

An old school of thought felt that love should be automatic. It believed that love which had to be pampered was no love at all. Frequently folks demonstrated more love for their dogs than for their mates.

We nurture plants. We pet gerbils. We coddle the boss. We humor storytellers. How much more sense it makes to romance the person we love!

The Song of Solomon was written primarily as a love letter. Its message is open, direct and almost embarrassing. The author has a high view of romance. We can almost feel the receiver's knees turn to mush when she reads it.

It isn't true that everyone needs only to *be* loved. That is not enough. Everyone needs to *feel* loved as well. Head knowledge won't cut it. If someone senses love, he feels valuable, wanted, needed, important. When a spouse says he would like to spend the evening with you, talk to you across a table, walk in the moonlight, take a boat ride, make love to you—you feel special.

Otherwise you wonder if you stay married because you wax linoleum well.

What Romance Costs

A happy husband told a group that he first dated his wife on the tenth of the month. For years now he has given her flowers on the tenth of each month. Where I live a single stem carnation still costs only $1.29. I saw roses recently for 99 cents each.

Another husband told us he has done the family grocery shopping for thirty-two years. It frees his wife up to do other things on Saturday and he has a ball rustling through the brussel sprouts. Pushing a shopping cart can be tremendously romantic.

Some couples go out to eat once a week no matter what. It's their chance to talk, connect and get their priorities straight. For others once a week would create a hardship. Often extra money is hard to come by. Romance doesn't have to be expensive, though. There aren't many couples who can't spring for coffee and donuts. In my town that's $1.10 with free refills on the coffee.

If you can put a few dollars together, a flight to some exotic location won't hurt a relationship either. A woman we know was facing a serious operation but she had some time before it had to be done. Her thoughtful husband pasted enough money together to take her to the Bahamas. They had a beautiful time in the sun, and she returned to face her surgery with new courage. It wasn't one of those absurd deals where you sell the farm; they just had to stretch a bit to reach their goal. But it paid off in love.

Pat and I occasionally have traveled the high road to romance. We have trekked through the jungles of Belize and made mad love in the Fort George Hotel. We've snuggled in the Everglades and watched the sun set in Key West. But we wouldn't trade anything for one simple five-dollar date we had. Our all-day ride into the Sandhills of Nebraska cost us just that much in gas. We turned the radio off, drove for hours to nowhere in particular and talked about nothing but each other. We've stayed in honeymoon suites that weren't as sexy as that.

Important Ingredients

The most important ingredient to effective romance is isolating yourselves and shutting out the normal world. Discussing utility bills seldom serves as an effective aphrodisiac.

Remember that aphrodisiacs are real. Oysters will

arouse you sexually. Mandrake leaves are a terrific turn-on. Chocolate in your Coke will get you panting. Anything is an aphrodisiac *if you believe* it is. Practically anything that will jump start your brain will put your body in gear. Certain smells, tastes, sights, memories are all potent if they work for you. There may be no scientific evidence for this, but what does science know about passion?

The key to romantic love is to find what turns the two of you on and do it—often. If violins churn your butter, great. If hang gliding turns your crank, go for it. If chicken wings prime his pump, buy a case. Romance will be one of the best investments you will ever make.

Here's a Romance Wheel for you. Check it frequently to see how well it is rolling.

Never apologize for being romantic. And don't worry about embarrassing the children; it makes them feel secure.

Flexercise

1. Write down three things that you consider romantic. Hand the list to your partner.

2. Plan one romantic surprise for your spouse. When can you spring it on him?

3. Prepare three coupons for your mate and deliver them.

Check
Your Baggage

A PSYCHOLOGIST ON THE RADIO offered this advice: "If the man you intend to marry has a poor relationship with his mother, give the ring back and run. He's going to take those problems out on you."

Certainly some truth lies in what he says, but it's laid out too black and white. All of us carry baggage, some good and some terrible. But we don't drop people merely because they have known trouble. That philosophy would keep all of us single.

Start out with three questions:

1. What has his experience been?
2. What is he doing to resolve the problem?
3. How will that problem disrupt your relationship?

Past Experience

Women who have been sexually abused usually bear carryover scars. They may tend to distrust men; they may avoid certain situations (parking lots, camping trips, or whatever reminds them of the abuse they suffered). But is that reason enough not to marry them?

One out of four women is molested seuxally before she turns sixteen. Are 25 percent of the females in our country disqualified from being married? That would be foolish.

Statistics say that the children of divorced parents are more likely to divorce. Ergo, it is unwise to marry someone from a divorced family.

Sorry it isn't that simple. Too many variables exist. I come from a divorced family. I definitely carry baggage from that poor relationship. But it wasn't sufficient reason for Pat to reject me. We recently celebrated our twenty-sixth anniversary.

All of us have faith in the healing process, in the power of growth, and in the ability to overcome obstacles. A person's experience is not enough of a criterion on which to eliminate him as a partner.

Improving

The second question, the crucial one, is, what is being done to resolve that conflict?

A person's baggage will cost his partner something. No doubt about that one. We may be up till 2 A.M. discussing the pain that strikes our spouse—but all of us do that. It's called the human condition. "For better or for worse" covers those 2 A.M. sessions.

Marriage partners who don't expect any 2 A.M. sessions are prime game for divorce. Unable to deal with problems, they want out at the first sign of smoke.

Granted, some nuts should never get married. But we can't disqualify them only because of a few bad experiences in the past. (We've all had our tough times.) A wide array of help is available, including education, support groups, counseling, Bible study and worship. By dealing progressively with the problem, a person makes an excellent candidate for a good partner.

Acknowledging the Luggage

Because bad baggage can hurt our relationship, it's important to admit its presence and move toward resolving it to protect our marriage. Ignoring the problem injures the love you have promised to each other.

Begin by looking at general categories:

1. Childhood traumas. Terrible experiences of abandonment by a parent, divorce, abuse, a death in the family, even illness or a handicap.

2. Poor relationships. Parents who refused to share themselves, spiteful grandparents, cruel teachers, rebellious siblings.

3. Destructive personal habits. Some have become dependent on gambling, alcohol or smoking (or even drugs) as an escape from reality. Others are heavily into shopping and debt as an attempt to alleviate the tension. Possibly they have the habit of disappearing for a day or two without telling anyone what is going on.

4. Personality traits. Many have developed a style which aggravates others. They tease, annoy, ridicule as efforts to gain attention. Often they do not realize their offensiveness but are simply relying on the poor personal skills they developed early and now find difficult to shake.

As usual, you might want to add to this list.

Loners do not heal as well as partners. We need each other. You are committed to your marriage; be commited to helping each other handle his baggage as well.

You may protest and insist, "My problems are *my* problems. I don't want to share them." Nothing could be further from the truth. In a marriage realtionship our difficulties hurt our partner. If we have no other reason to deal with our own baggage, we *must* do it out of love for our mate.

We will never clean out our baggage until we experience spiritual cleansing. Without the partners' accepting the forgiveness of Jesus Christ, some marriages will always be cluttered with junk from the past. How often have you seen the pain in the faces of couples merely because they refuse God's mercy and grace?

Couples who fooled around or became pregnant before they got married may still accuse each other. A partner may have wasted the money away, lost the business and said something terribly insulting. Because either person refuses to accept forgiveness from the other or from God, these couples continue to drain the energy from their marriage — it is burning out for lack of forgiveness.

The Bible tells me to put my baggage down because "he has been cleansed from his past sins" (2 Peter 1:9). If I deny the grace of God, I tend to tear up my wheels from friction.

People with problems *can* live well together, but those who help each other to resolve the problems live even better together.

Identifying the Luggage

Most baggage can be placed into four categories. Although these are oversimplified, I can use them easily as tools to help me get a handle on my feelings.

Stored baggage

Even the best of us will die with some unresolved history: a cantankerous uncle who will *never* be our friend, verbal abuse in our past that we may never wipe clean, or _____ (you fill in the blank). We would like to be totally optimistic, but evil has too firm a grip on us to allow us complete freedom. Even the best spiritual life will probably never erase every blemish.

Mixed baggage

Mixed baggage resolves itself on some days and is disastrous on others. People with severe low self-esteem find periods when they function well and ride on top of the waves, but most of the time they feel like a surfer who's just been wiped out. When we open the suitcase we never quite know what might be inside.

This baggage makes us the victim. Its contents can do whatever it wants to us on any given day. Because the situation is not improving, it can always turn hostile. It is the unpredictable part of our past that we have chosen not to deal with effectively.

Donna's father abandoned her when she was six and has never returned. Most days she ignores it and goes on with her married life. But because she has refused to work her feelings through, this history can rear its head and strike her any time. It's mixed baggage because it has dormant force which can explode in a destructive manner. Some days Donna learns from it, and her father's betrayal makes her a better parent. Other days a sense of having been coldly, totally rejected overwhelms her and she wants to fight back with her own brand of coldness. Unfortunately she never knows how this worm will turn.

Baggage in Process

This is the luggage that is being sorted. Not simply being sorted and resorted, but rather being dealt with and assigned to meaningful resting places. Cabinets, drawers, closets, attics are filled with parts of our past that have been resolved.

In mixed baggage the contents are frequently handled but seldom put in the proper place. Once our baggage has reached this process stage, our history finds its correct place in our lives.

Christmas Baggage

Not all baggage is grim or dismal. Every Christmas my

wife's relatives send Christmas packages brimming with goodies. There are chocolates, kitchen untensils, novelties, games, calendars, gloves. Each layer in the box brings new surprises and more fun.

There are no incriminations in the box. No unpleasant memories or sad messages. The contents are happy.

Most of us can draw this kind of cheerfulness from somewhere in our past. Maybe you had a loving grand-mother or an understanding, encouraging teacher. Count this as a piece of big, fat, shiny Christmas baggage, a gift that is all your own.

Love Gift

There is no greater pledge we can give to the person we love than this: "I will work on my baggage as a gift of love to you, my partner."

Anything we can do to:

> reduce our fears
> minimize our prejudice
> handle our anger
> increase our humility
> accept forgiveness
> learn to forgive
> find peace with our past
> accept ourselves
> find reconciliation

> will add strength to our relationship.

Flexercise

---

1. Is there one piece of mixed baggage you would like to handle? Have you ever discussed it with anyone?

2. Have you shared your baggage with your part-ner? What was his reaction?

3. Describe some of your "Christmas baggage."

What Does She Mean?

Y OU COULD SEE the frustration in Judy's reddened eyes. "I never know if I am supposed to say anything. If I tell him what I really want, I feel pushy and demanding. No, I don't want to go fishing on our vacations, but if I say anything, I come across as a witch."

It's a servant-syndrome which says she feels strongly about some things but is reluctant to say so directly. She wants to hint, sprinkle clues around, and gently move the rudder, but she wants to never say, "I would like this and not that."

Not all women are indirect communicators. Some are abrasively rude in their directness, but many have found a happy balance. When women do camouflage their communication, they slow the process and strain the relationship. Their goal is to keep unnecessary stress off their marriage, but in all probability they accomplish only the opposite.

Normally the indirect communicator suffers from one or more of the following problems:

1. She doesn't think she is personally worthy enough to receive what she wants.

2. She doubts her ability to get her point across well.

3. She has little faith in her husband and is afraid
    he will reject her and her requests.

These all may be false beliefs, or there may be some
truth in her assessment of the situation. Whether fact or
fiction, though, each of these conclusions drains vitality
from the marriage. Instead of adding essential fuel to the
relationship, the fear and uncertainty burn off good energy and weaken the intimacy.

Jeff and Nancy

Jeff described the typical date with his wife Nancy this
way: "We decide to go out to dinner, but by the time we get
in the car the tension has begun to mount. I don't want to
name the restaurant for fear I'll pick some place Nancy
thinks is too expensive or too far away. She won't name the
place for fear she comes across as bossy.

"More than once we have driven for five or ten miles,
felt the frustration grow and then simply turned around
and driven home. Of course it hurts our marriage. It robs
us of good times. And it's all so dumb."

If we can identify indirect communication early in our
marriage, it is far easier to correct. But many of us have
practiced it for ten or fifteen years and have bruised an important nerve. We now find it hard to trust what the other
person says. It is difficult to believe a person who has played
verbal charades with us that long.

Fortunately, it's not impossible to move toward healthy communication. However, the couple must feel that the
change is worth the effort because they have become fairly comfortable with non-communication. They also must
have a love for each other which makes the transition important.

Imagine the frustration. John calls and wants to play
chess. I'd love to do that but my wife and I have discussed
going out for the evening. I'd love that even more. The
problem is I'm not sure she really wants to go. I tell John

to hold the phone while I double-check.

I hurry into the kitchen and ask Pat if we are going out tonight.

She says, "Oh, you go ahead and play chess."

Now I have no idea what is going on. Does she want to go to dinner? Or does she have things she needs to do at home? Or is she simply being generous? Or does she think I'd rather play chess? Or what in the world is happening? Boy, I hate that.

Making It a Point to Care

Repeat this to yourself: A person who doesn't care brings injury to his marriage.

Read it again.

To acquiesce continuously is to become less and less a full person. A healthy marriage needs two complete people. If one partner is called upon to make all the decisions, that partner becomes too expansive. He is calling all the shots for another perfectly competent person. The imbalance of one person being in control and the other being passive will cause the ship of marriage to list badly. Vessels which list badly do not sail well in good weather and often sink during storms.

If you have trouble saying exactly what you want, you might begin to improve by narrowing your choices. To say you don't care where you eat is too formless to handle. The next time a decision has to be made you might help by saying, "I'd enjoy either Chop-Stick Charlie's or Barnacle Ben's Fish House. Why don't you pick one of those? This will allow you to reduce the field, express your opinions and still avoid feeling too aggressive.

Practice the "narrowing technique" until it becomes comfortable. From there you can eventually leap to, "My appetite is calling for Angie's Chicken Joint if that's all right with you."

Kindness dictates that we usually decide together. Unfortunately, that doesn't work well if one person always bails out of the decision-making process.

Making a List Available

Picture your partner gathering fuel to keep your marriage warm and crackling. He looks over the fuels that are usable. There is wood, coal, electricity, gas, propane and whatever else. He is happy to deliver whatever works. He simply wants to know what kind of system you are on. Help him by describing exactly what it takes to maintain your temperature.

Margaret explained. "I hate to see Tony's birthday come around. He's impossible to please. He doesn't want neckties or fishing equipment. If I get him a pen it usually isn't the right one and ends up in a drawer. Why doesn't he just say what he would like?"

Have you ever tried to hang a jacket on a loose wall hook? Every time you put the jacket on the hook, the hook swings around and the coat drops to the floor. There is nothing to get hold of.

Do your spouse a favor. Tell him what you want.

This list doesn't have to be written down, though that works well, but at least it should be expressed verbally.

Tell your husband:

> You like flowers (under $5).
> Simple earrings are appreciated.
> You don't want kitchen utensils.
> A neat nightie would be nice.
> Pie and coffee make a good date.

Be specific. Be reasonable. Be direct. Be thankful. Be helpful.

Practical Principles

In looking for constructive guidelines, we frequently turn to the Bible to get our bearings. Here are a handful of principles that have worn well with time.

1. Use Sincerity

The Bible says love must be sincere (Romans 12:9). Sincerity doesn't have to be rude, but it doesn't play games either. The closer our partner comes to understanding how we really feel, the less tension and anxiety will exist in our relationship.

2. Use Yes and No

Don't waste time trying to be ambiguous hoping the problem will go away. If he wants to go break dancing and your clavicle is in traction, say no, and explain. Otherwise he has to guess why you are being evasive (Matthew 5:37).

3. Use Kindness

If you are going to reject the idea, let him down easily. Think of how you would like to have your plan turned down. On the other hand, it is not kind to encourage behavior which you actually do not want. Love is kind (1 Corinthians 13:4).

4. Use Encouragement

Love at its best does not pounce on people and leave them in a crushed heap. If there are things you don't want to do, suggest something you both might enjoy. Separate the activity you are rejecting from the person you are accepting. Don't assume he knows that. Make it perfectly clear. "Your love has given me great joy and encouragement" (Philemon 7).

5. Change

Often we throw up our hands and say, "What's the use? I am nondirect, insecure and a tad evasive. After all these years I am too entrenched to change." Many of us feel that way but the facts beg to differ. We can change, and many do.

- First, we must know the facts and recognize what

is going on.

- Second, we acknowledge how our behavior is counterproductive to our relationship.

- Third, we find information on how we might begin to change. Some of that information is contained in this chapter and book.

- Fourth, we ask God to help us put some of this material to practical use.

Realizing that we will not totally change, we aim to become 10 percent, 25 percent, 75 percent better. Those who do change will help guarantee a long and meaningful marriage relationship.

Flexercise

1. What type of situations do you have trouble talking about? Do you know why that is?

2. Are there some barriers to open expression in your marriage? Name one.

3. How could you improve in letting your spouse know just what you mean?

Guessing How Your Husband Feels

W HAT DOES SILENCE tell us? Does it mean the person is happy, angry, content, or merely thinking about an old girlfriend? While some of us have learned to interpret a measured silence by our partner, most of us are left in a quandary, trying to guess what is going on in that jellied computer called a brain.

With all the talk about the modern "sensitive" male we would think that communication was flowing between couples like clear, gentle mountain streams. Unfortunately, that is probably wishful thinking. While men may have reached new heights of fluidness discussing things like baseball, hockey, auto racing, politics and water gauges, there is reason to believe he still locks his jaws when it comes to feelings.

Feelings As Fuel

His inability or refusal to talk on the gut level robs the relationship of needed vital fuel. He needs to feed the marriage by contributing his feelings because her feelings are not enough to keep their intimacy alive.

"No wonder the marriage didn't work," Sue told me. "He was always upset if I didn't tell him how I felt, but I was supposed to read his mind to know how he felt."

It is impossible to understand a person if we do not

connect with his feelings. We can map his actions; we can observe his choices; but we have not fathomed the person until we know what lights up his emotional circuit. Does his wife understand how he feels when certain subjects are brought up? If not, she is handicapped in trying to develop a full relationship.

Why He Holds Back

As a male he has been trained well to withhold his emotions. His manhood usually has been measured on his ability to disguise his feelings. Men who cry don't get promoted. Men who express outrage at racial injustice are considered unstable. Men who are too romantic are not treated as one of the boys.

Practically every expression of manhood he sees tells him to swallow his emotions. Athletes, movie heroes, business leaders, military officers and store managers are all depicted as tough, tight-lipped and stern.

Despite their protests to the contrary, women also seem afraid their men will become "mushy." They are used to dealing with taciturn statues and aren't sure they want a change.

Society, parents and wives are telling the men to be tough. Consequently many of them who want to be tender move toward homosexuality because they think there they can stop being Mr. Macho.

The pressure to bottle up our emotions is almost unbearable, and it works. The overwhelming majority of men in the United States express their feelings to no one. We are an emotional desert.

A friend told me that's exactly what his wife wants him to be, an emotional wasteland.

"If I get sick," he said, "she wants me to go to bed and suffer silently. She brings me food and hurries out of the room. It's not that she is uncaring. I've watched her nurse the children back to health. She doctors the cats forever.

But somehow she can't face her husband as sick or vulnerable.

"That puts me in a fix to buck up and act like a man. With that kind of situation, you tend to keep your emotions hidden."

Bringing About Change

It's tough to change another person, especially if he is not looking for change. Don't expect a new person, but aim for 10 or 20 percent more emotional expression.

Several approaches are possible. Here are a few that might hold promise:

nagging	atmosphere
demands	education
permission	motivation
example	encouragement

Consider briefly the strengths and faults of each.

Nagging

Probably the least effective. It tends to frighten a man into a hole and understandably keeps him there. He builds resistance, and like a body on a starvation diet, he begins to fight back.

The dictionary sees nagging as gnawing, complaining, scolding, incessant fault-finding, badgering. None of these seem particularly appealing.

Demands

Many impatient types want to square off and tell him to shape up right now. They believe in the direct approach and immediate results.

Remember, he is facing centuries of tradition. We don't simply tell cats to leave the birds alone. Men face an emotional maze which they don't fully comprehend. By demanding immediate and radical change, we may close his doors forever.

Permission

Change takes place most easily when it has the approval of those the person counts as important. He may have trouble reading the signals you are sending. Do you want him to "close up and be a man" or "open up and be a person"?

In straightforward, unequivocal terms he needs to know it is okay to open up. You can handle it and would welcome it. It will be risky for him to open up, and he needs to know his feelings are safe and acceptable with you, no matter what those feelings may be.

Example

He needs examples from two sources. **One,** he has to see his spouse opening up her emotions. We will not be successful in bringing others out while we stay in.

Two, he needs to know about other men who share their feelings. Subtly remind him of those you admire who do. Don't use examples which are too close or threatening. Uncles, football coaches and business leaders make excellent subjects.

By citing them with approval you send a powerful indirect message.

Atmosphere

Each of us needs a safe place to express ourselves. Sometimes these are public places like restaurants. Many couples share coffee and talk about intimate subjects with a remarkable amount of privacy. The right restaurant can be nonthreatening and yet isolated enough to be personal. Millions of marriages grow in precisely this atmosphere.

Others thrive at home alone after the children go to bed or while the couple is in bed.

Don't push for emotional exposure while in a group or at a party. Some attempt this in hope of pressuring him to express himself. It usually backfires and makes the situation worse.

Education

Leave articles and books in a place where they might be read. Watch television shows which discuss feelings. Attend a seminar addressing the feelings of couples. (Remember, don't overdo this one.)

It is unlikely that he understands the damage he is doing. It is equally unlikely that he will believe all of it from his wife. Slide the facts close to him and pray he will learn.

Motivation

Why should a man change? Why would a man leave a familiar harbor and strike out for one with uncertain danger? Will he do it merely because you told him to?

Explain the benefits. Your marriage needs it. Your love for each other can only grow. You can't provide all the emotional fuel. Your son or daughter will find it easier to deal with their feelings if they see their father sharing his. When times get tough, your relationship will be stronger if you can say how you feel.

Most likely he doesn't believe his silence adversely affects anyone else. Conversely he believes that by opening up he might hurt everyone. Let him know how it really is.

Encouragement

Permission says, "You may say it." Encouragement says, "I'm thrilled you brought it out." When he opens up, gently lead him on to say more. Don't interrogate or probe him but add comments which will keep the flow coming, such as:

How does that make you feel?

Have you ever told them? Why?

Do you ever feel there is something you want to get out?

I love you all the more.

This helps me understand.

Avoid "shut down" questions. Aim for open-ended comments that make him want to share more. Likewise steer clear of interrogative questions where he might feel he is being grilled or pumped. We sound like detectives when our questions:

> *Demand an answer:* "Let's get to the bottom of this" or "I need to know this now."
>
> *Are harsh in tone:* "Aren't you tired of keeping this in?"
>
> *Smack of accusation:* "You could get help if you wanted to" or "Are you using your problem to keep a distance between us?"
>
> *Sound unsympathetic:* "Doesn't everyone have problems?"
>
> "I know just what you are going through."
>
> "My brother's problem was bigger than yours."
>
> "Why don't you just shake it off?"
>
> "I know what I would have done."
>
> *Are interrogative:* "Why didn't you tell him off?"
>
> "Why didn't you move out?"
>
> "You should have gone to the police."
>
> "Did you have sex with her?"
>
> "Why didn't you complain?"
>
> "How long did you put up with that?"

Do you know how your husband feels when he hears the following words?

debt	affair	pain
lonely	intimate	fired
impotent	laughter	anger
fear	mother	father

The list could be longer but, keeping the preceding approaches in mind, you could use some of these to get a discussion going.

Stereotypes

This is basically a male problem, but we have made it almost exclusively that. In doing this we run the danger of being stereotypical. Actually many women share the same problem — they are choking on their own emotions. These same principles apply to them.

However, though women have some trouble expressing themselves, they are used-car salesmen compared to our he-man types. The inability to express feelings is still predominantly a male situation. Any list of marital difficulties will show poor communication at or near the top, and more often than not the husband is at the core of this malfunction.

Remaining Strangers

The old saw tells us we all marry strangers. As hard as that might be to accept, the saddest reality is that after twenty years of marriage many women are still married to strangers. That's almost — not quite, but almost — like not being married. You share a bed, you share the bills, you might even bowl together, but you remain emotionally distanced.

People who do not bind emotionally are not sure how their partner will react under crisis. Consequently there remains an instability. If he keeps his own counsel, his wife cannot measure the severity of his panic, his fear or his insecurity. Neither can she appreciate his dreams, hopes or happiness. This lack of understanding can make her wonder, *When tough times come, which way will he respond?* Since he is a stranger, she cannot feel even reasonably assured as to how dependable he will be.

We use Proverbs 31 to discuss the virtuous woman, but look again. The husband in that chapter isn't moldy cheese.

He expresses himself well and often. She knows how he feels and that frees her to venture out. They who know each other well make a good team.

Look at a bit of what she does:

> She knows he has full confidence in her (verse 11).
>
> She can buy land on her own (verse 16).
>
> Her husband calls her blessed and praises her (verse 28).
>
> Even though he expresses his feelings, he is never considered a wimp. He takes his place at the city gate with respect and is considered one of the elders in the land (verse 23).
>
> She knows how he feels and she knows where she stands. This jewel is no longer married to a protective, insecure stranger. They understand each other.

Jesus Christ wasn't an emotional blank, either. He wasn't Rambo; he wasn't even *Christ*bo. He wept; He was angry; He was disappointed, discouraged, happy. He felt for children, cared for parents, and forgave the injured. No man has to feel apologetic for sharing His emotions.

Flexercise

---

1. How does your husband handle his emotions?

2. Where would you most like to see him improve in expressing his emotions?

3. What is one way you could help him express his feelings?

Marriage Turnover

O N A RECENT television show, an actress explained that her mother had dumped her father and married a childhood sweetheart. The appreciative audience broke into hearty applause while the show's host beamed with approval.

Without any apparent twinge of conscience, they thunderously supported the death of a marriage. Who cares what happened to husband number one? What concern could they have for the first failed relationship? They were carried away by the superficial notion that some great romantic cause had been served.

The New Semester Syndrome

Presently a theme is being promoted that if your marriage is burning out for any reason, it's time to get a new stove. After all there is no point in putting up with a low flame. In some circles the new heroes are the people who have trashed their marriages and found other partners. Many of us admire them because secretly we want to do the same from time to time.

I call it the "new semester syndrome." About halfway through each semester in school, behind, confused, and in despair, I always wanted to jump out and start the next semester. If I could only begin fresh, I knew I could do better next time. Fortunately, the school always made me stick it out and do better where I was.

The fallacy of the new semester syndrome is borne out by some discouraging statistics. Second marriages presently have the same (or higher) divorce rate as first marriages. Could it be that if we do not resolve our personal conflicts in our first marriage, we carry them into our second?

There is no doubt that some have found ecstasy in their second relationship. But not usually.

Some couples have been able to make their first marriage their second marriage. After five or ten years they wised up to their problems and changed dramatically. They identified their destructive behavior and adjusted their course before they burned out.

Having Your Affair

The statistics revealing how many people would like to have an affair should set off alarms in our brain. We are looking for something new, something exciting, something adventurous, something romantic, something even risky — and we don't think we can get it at home.

But many of us would like to have an affair at home. We would like to escape the routine. We want to get turned on again rather than used. We want to step outside our hassle over bills, children and cleaning. Every now and then we would like to steal away and have a rendezvous with the person we married.

Wanting to Jump Ship

A new partner would be a myth — even if you already knew him. You would not have married the new person just to find out what he would be like under the pressure of daily living. So let's look at the person you do share a roof with and make a list about him.

Make a list of only three to five things you'd like to see changed. I'm sure you sometimes feel you could list forty, but that probably wouldn't help. A long list is overwhelming and frequently exaggerated. First get the list down to bite size. You can make another list after this first group becomes manageable.

After you write the important goals down, think them over. There's no point in spending your energy on trifling matters like who reads the funnies first. Be sure your goals are real to you.

The next day sit down with your spouse and approach him or her with your priorities. He may not like everything you have written down, but he doesn't have to.

Say something like:

> "These things are really hurting me. I need you to help me with them"; or,

> "This is my list of things that bother me. I wish you would make your own list and show it to me"; or,

> "I need your help. Could we work on these things together?"

Don't joke, flinch or look at the floor. Be clear-eyed and direct. Don't be harsh or mean. Be friendly but firm. Your spouse needs to know you are burning out and need relief.

What if your spouse gets angry? Anger isn't all bad. If he is not a violent person, a bit of fury can be constructive. You are angry, too, and smothering your feelings. Your spouse may need to feel some of that as well. Don't let his anger throw you. The loud voice, red face, slow grind or pouting are surface matters but they are not the problem. Try to stay calm when your partner flares up. He has given you a good indication of how he feels. Even though it is difficult, reach beyond the surface and say something like:

"Tell me why this bothers you."

"You don't like it; how can we work it out?"

"There must be other ways to do this; let's talk about it."

"I'll be here if you would like to air this out."

"We have options, Baby. Let's look for them."

More likely he will be embarrassed, defensive, maybe accusatory. He also might become humble, sensitive, compassionate. If some confrontation is not made, your marriage will shrivel and shrink. You will probably shrink with it. The best chance your marriage has is today. None of us should let it die because we are afraid to face our situation.

Feeling Restless

How many things have we done without knowing why? We have changed wallpaper, bought a new car, run away for the evening—and we can't pinpoint the reason. We feel restless and we don't understand it. Like an animal with a worm in its brain we start to wander, aimlessly and hopelessly.

We feel a craving for change. It's illogical and undefinable but the feeling is real. Unable to isolate the internal cause we imagine that external alterations will make the gnawing go away. That's when we hope a new apartment, a new job, a new city, a new spouse will cure what ails us. It won't, but millions of us try it.

After we make the "big switch," drag through the agony of divorce, remarriage, relocation and readjustment, we feel something creeping up like cheap underwear. It's that same old feeling of restlessness. Since we didn't deal with it, it didn't go away. Restlessness is real, and it is internal.

Restlessness can be chemical, psychological, physical, emotional and spiritual. It is never cured by changing license plates. Our best bet is to work out the uneasiness with the people who love us. If moving is in order, you'd best move together.

Bible verses are like grass seed. There is no point in just throwing them around, but a few planted strategically could produce well. Plant this little beauty in your yard:

**Find rest, O my soul, in God alone;
my hope comes from him** (Psalm 62:5).

Restlessness is not healed by a change of scenery. The cure begins with a change of heart.

Victim Position

Often we play games by trying to wiggle ourselves into the victim posture. We perceive ourselves as too nice to terminate our marriage so we begin to jockey for position. Our goal is to force our spouse into rejecting us. To that end we act in a repulsive but nonaggressive fashion. By feeding negative energy into our relationship we hope to provoke our partner into taking aggressive action. That gets us off the hook and turns him or her into the bad guy. You've heard of it.

Allen wanted a quiet way to provoke his wife so he developed a meek, irritating style that would drive her crazy. When asked if he wanted to go someplace or do something, he mumbled a noncommittal, "I don't care." When asked what was wrong, he uttered a dreary, drawn out, "Nothing."

By dropping down to a barely audible voice and a prenatal attitude, he sets up his wife to blow her cool. If she falls for the trap and explodes, or otherwise reacts emotionally, it proves to him that he is the victim. She can't win. He has taken control by giving up.

Consequently he can't be accused of doing anything wrong. He isn't doing anything. Allen has put her into a position where she is likely to look bad at any turn.

Allen is playing hardball. He is set up to guarantee he will become a victim. Once that is completed he can demand reparation or payment because he has become victimized.

Not that Allen is unique. Many men, and women as well, are masters at this cruel game.

When we take a victim posture, we invite serious injury to our relationship. We need to become aware when we are using this technique, and then discard it immediately. Open and caring confrontation is a thousand percent improvement over this deceitful and wimpish form of combat.

In its extreme, the victim is looking for an excuse to leave. Unable to fight or take flight, he pushes for a cause that will force him out and allow him to switch trains.

We waste our energies plotting ways to get out of our marriage. We misuse our fantasies dreaming of what it must be like to live with someone else. Far better to redouble our efforts to reorganize our present arrangement and deal with our real problems. Begin plotting how to keep the marriage going. Instead of planning a rendezvous with a new lover, why not rent a motel room for the partner you have? A divorce lawyer could cost $1000 or more. Taking your spouse out to dinner one night a week will cost less than $40 a week and might save your marriage. A real deal.

If you find it awkward to talk to your husband, think of the pain of getting to know a new person. Prepare for conversations with your spouse as you would with a date. Think through what small gift would cause your partner's eyes to sparkle: a box of mints, a new book, a magazine, rent a movie especially for her. Take a fresh look at what might make the evening special.

Millions try it every year and are able to revitalize their marriages.

Flexercise

1. What could you do this week to add new vitality to your marriage?

2. Have you ever thought of leaving your spouse? Why didn't you?

3. If you present a list of needed improvements in your relationship, what might be two things on the list? Why haven't you presented it?

B*udget or* B*urn* U*p*

I
F MARRIAGE HAD A TOOTHACHE, it would be
money. For most couples finances represent a low-
grade, constant pain that occasionally flares up into
absolute agony. Much of that misery is caused by our failure
to get a handle on money management.

Brad grew to see his difficulty in realistic terms. "It
didn't make any difference how much money we made—
and we had some good years—but no matter what, we were
always broke and anxious, and we bickered over where the
money went. Sometimes you wish someone could come in
and take over your finances."

Since almost every survey puts money problems near
the head of marriage stress, you might imagine that we
would work hard to conquer this mountain. Instead, the
well-educated, sophisticated, cool generation continues to
treat money like a great mystery box.

What We Need

There are several reasons we handle finances poorly.
Here are just a few to get us thinking:

1. We have almost no training in personal finances.
2. Some of us consider money evil and face it only
   begrudgingly.
3. Many are social climbers and are philosophical-
   ly dedicated to spending it all.

4. Others have a low view of life and refuse to
   prepare for tomorrow.

From these basic flaws grow more complications than we can track. If we treat cars with this much abuse, they fall apart. If we ignore our children this much, they turn into apes. It is a wonder that any marriage survives the strain of financial neglect.

A marriage has a distinct advantage when the couple can handle finances in a positive way. To do this requires an attribute called levelheadedness.

Levelheaded couples aggressively take control of their money.

There is pleasure and a sense of accomplishment when marriage partners put their finances to good use. The opposite is distress when they try to figure out how their money evaporated.

I have a friend who loves to handle his money. Each week when he gets his pay check, he divides it into different compartments. So much goes to recreation, so much to clothes, so much to pay off the refrigerator. Systematically he enjoys watching his money go to work. When the refrigerator is paid off, he intends to purchase a golf cart. Chuck isn't miserly, stashing every dime to build up his estate; neither is he foolishly wearing blinders. He is just dividing up his check into progressive, growing areas.

Many of us are reticent to try this because we are afraid, fearful we don't know what we are doing. Since we have no experience, we are afraid we will mishandle it. If we run away from our money, we *will* mishandle it.

Every once in a while we meet a couple on a modest income who seem to have so many neat things. They have a boat, maybe a cabin; they have been to Europe and their children are dressed like catalog models. They enjoy managing their money, and in the long run they have more and do more than some with twice their income.

Levelheaded couples know money is not evil.

Too many of us see money as one of those rotten odors in life that we have to tolerate. Money is not the cure-all some believe it to be, but neither is it the drooling monster some Christians have painted. It is neutral.

It does not become power or corruption or a blessing until you and I decide what we will make it. Spirituality and finances are comfortable bedfellows if both are treated with respect. The Bible does not say money is the root of all evil — it says the *love* of money is (1 Timothy 6:10). God will not be disappointed because we handled our money well.

Levelheaded couples do not burn out trying to get rich.

The classic picture of the modern American couple is two people running frantically in different directions as they scramble for upper middle-class status. All meaningful relationships are forfeited in this relentless drive.

Some couples put all of their fulfillment into the chase for bigger and better. When they finally arrive, exhausted but well-heeled, they discover they failed to grow with each other and their marriage has fallen apart.

A number of famous athletes seem to have followed this pattern. Only they know what really happened. They chased fame, hired agents, sacrificed time and reached the pinnacle of their careers. Within months of their success a "spokesman" announced that the pair separated. The hunt was over and they had nothing left for each other.

While the couple is in this race for super mobility, they pretend it is no problem. And it may not be. But when they slow down and face the partner, the emptiness becomes apparent. It's too bad because they might have loved each other had they only taken the time to find out.

The sound biblical principle is found in Proverbs 23:4:

**Do not wear yourself out to get rich;
have the wisdom to show restraint.**

Levelheaded couples get a handle on their debt.

Debt is not the curse of the earth. Unmanageable debt might be. The question is, can we control our borrowing in a way that it cannot get out of hand?

The important rule of thumb is that, **first**, the two of you discuss your attitude toward debt, and reach an agreement. **Second**, you add up how much your debt costs you. (This is especially important now that less interest can be deducted from taxes.) **Third**, ask what realistic provision you have made in case something unexpected happens and you do not have enough to make a payment.

Agreement, factual information, reserve — don't buy a rocking chair until you have resolved these three issues.

Read *Your Money Matters* by Malcolm MacGregor, Bethany House, chapters 8 and 9.

If you listen to contemporary couples, they seem to be saying, "We can always sell the house." "We can always declare bankruptcy." "We can always double our mortgage." What we don't hear is how many marriages split under that kind of upheaval. Love is fragile enough without having financial bombs going off here and there.

Type the following verses and paste them into your checkbook:

"The borrower is servant to the lender"
(Proverbs 22:7).

"The wicked borrow and do not repay"
(Psalm 37:21).

Levelheaded couples have joint control over their finances.

In the old days husbands managed the money and simply told the little lady not to worry about it. If that approach ever did work, it doesn't today. Neither partner thrives on ignorance and both should feel secure in the knowledge of what is going on.

● Each partner should feel assured that his contribution to the financial stability of the home is essential. This is equally true if she works exclusively at home. Her expense-cutting measures are a substantial help.

- Husband and wife each must have disposable income for which neither is accountable. She should not have to justify every magazine she buys or he each sleeve of golf balls. Their disposable money should be written into the budget, however, so it does not unknowingly mushroom.

- Neither spouse should make a sizable purchase without consulting the other. Men who buy $400 toys without preparing their wives may be creating an insecure atmosphere.

Not being in total control of the money will present a threat to the manhood of some men. If so, they misunderstand the true quality of a man and have confused it with machismo. Men can rise up and share.

Discuss joint control of money early. Disagreement on this point creates more havoc than most any other issue.

Levelheaded couples give money away.

It's fun to give money away. When done wisely, you gain the satisfaction of knowing you are helping others and serving God.

Couples who are dedicated to collecting and hoarding money establish an introverted and miserly outlook on life. Many married partners eventually suffer under the tedium of self-centeredness.

Smart couples give responsibly. They know the integrity of the group they are giving to or through. They develop a system of giving because it allows them to give more.

A group I belong to was formed explicitly to give money away. We reach out to others and buy food, supply college money, pay auto repairs, furnish clothing, operate a food exchange, or whatever. Each Sunday we all meet before church and decide where to distribute cash and other gifts. We believe in the joy of giving.

Jesus Christ has filled us with love which needs a way to flow outward. Finances are part of that outflow. We can't stash enough money to catch up with our rich neighbors anyway, so we might as well enjoy the pleasure of giving.

Paste these verses on your calculator:

"God loves a cheerful giver"
(2 Corinthians 9:7).

"He who gives to the poor will lack nothing"
(Proverbs 28:27).

Levelheaded couples create a budget.

Linda told me, "I thought I was spending $20 or $25 a week on extras until I took the time to write it down. The total was closer to $75. That woke me up to reality."

Without some kind of system, our finances may already have become a runaway train without our realizing it. *Budget* is an ugly word, much like *Tax Form* or *Instructions to Assemble.* Overcoming our fear of using a budget system can save us from a continuous headache, and it may show us we have more usable income than we thought.

Begin with a simple A-B-C step. Move to the more complicated technicalities later, if ever. No one knows for sure what your budget should be. Much of it depends on how you want to live. However, start by listing the areas where your money must go. The first few percentages listed here are merely sweeping suggestions. Adjust them to fit your situation, then fill in the rest appropriately, keeping the total at no more than 100 percent.

Housing, utilities and upkeep	25-30%
Auto payment/operation/maintenance .	15-18%
Food and supplies	18-20%
Giving	5-10%

Clothing . . . .

Retirement/investment savings . . . . .

Medical . . . .

Insurances . . . .

Installment payments . . . .

Entertainment . . . .

Vacation . . . .

Spread the percentages over the items in the list according to your lifestyle and taste. Now you have a handle on where your money goes. If you need to increase a percentage, remember, you must subtract an amount from somewhere else and keep the total at no more than 100.

Once you have translated the percentages into dollars, you may find you are spending more money than shows on the list. If so, call it "Money through the cracks." It's important to find out where that money is going and account for it. Most money should be spent consciously.

First, if there are other categories, list them. Don't break them down, yet. Lump both cars together. Don't divide her clothes from his. Too many of us bog down arguing over the details.

Second, list all of your total income, both male and female, together. Then divide the totals into the percentages noted above.

Great idea. The only problem is, your percentages won't match those listed. No need to panic. Simply adjust them to agree with what you are spending. After writing down the percentages, put exact dollar amounts next to each one. This will reveal about how much you are spending and where. At a quick glance you can see which categories are draining too much and which ones call for more.

Take time to get used to the general categories. Once you feel comfortable with them, go to specifics. For examaple, separate the clothing group into his, hers and the kids. Spell out the entertainment or vacation you can plan.

Your first reaction may be that you just don't make enough money. Most people probably feel this way. The good news is that you can begin to make realistic adjustments and put your money to maximum benefit.

Once your finances have come into focus, you should look for a book dealing solely with money. There are easy-to-read, helpful volumes on the market designed precisely for you.

The apostle Paul told the Corinthians to handle their money in an orderly fashion (1 Corinthians 16:2). They were to put a certain amount aside and save it until his visit so they wouldn't be faced with a sudden cash crisis. Money management has much to recommend it. On the other hand, financial chaos can only hurt us.

Flexercise

Here's a checklist to help you control your money.

Credit cards are dangerous.

* Keep good tax records—it's almost like a third income.

* Fix it yourself when you can.

How many things do you do for fun, for free?

Credit cards are dangerous.

Cutting back on good food is no savings.

* Keep a balanced checkbook.

* Help your friends on projects (and they might help you).

Credit cards are dangerous.

What is your present trend? (Are you losing money, gaining, staying even, or don't you know?)

* These are your action points for this chapter.

Working Too Hard at Your Marriage

D O YOU EVER GET THE FEELING your marriage
has been studied to death? Are you tired of having
sex 2.2 times a week and aiming for 2.6 children?
Are you exhausted from chasing every marriage fad like
matching jogging suits and joint yoga classes?

Are you bored from watching talk shows discuss com-
patibility tests, open marriage and how to tell if your husband has been cheating? Have you had your marriage diced
into six predictable stages so you can tell what will happen
during each year of your life together?

Some helps are beneficial and certainly have con-
tributed to the quality of our married lives. We would be
foolish to ignore the assistance that is available. But, unfortunately, many of us have begun to suffer from a mas-
sive overload. We are getting too much information from
too many sources, much of it contradictory and sometimes
incorrect.

Many of us need to give it a rest.

The two extremes are: (1) to ignore our marriage, cross
our fingers and hope it works out; and (2) to reduce it to a
sociology class, chart our relationship and look for the
demographic drifts.

Not only are we worn out from professional advice, but
often our friends also have pelted us with their corrective

little gems. These people are well-meaning, and they always know "exactly" what we are going through, but . . .

There isn't enough fuel in the universe to support a perfect marriage. Relax and give love a chance.

Our marriages can last extremely well even if he falls asleep on the couch, she hangs hose in the shower, and he spends too much money on a remote control car. It's called flexibility, individualism and expression. Couples flourish on it. Smart couples learn to appreciate imperfection. They even manage to laugh about it.

There is nothing wrong with men who watch football all day. Women who park the car across the line in the garage frequently make acceptable mothers. Wives who nag about the lawn can be great lovers.

Marriage-envy

The unexamined life may not be worth living but the overexamined marriage is a genuine pain.

"It seemed like all we did was try to be like other couples," John complained. "If anyone mentioned flowers, dinner, a movie, camping, walking, push-ups or ballooning, we were off and chasing dreams. You would think we had no life of our own. Whatever other couples said was good for their marriage automatically became part of ours.

"Our own marriage, our interests, our romance was never enough. We kept comparing, envying and conforming. Envy of other marriages was a put-down of ours. After a while I didn't want to try anymore."

Marriage-envy is a dangerous game that none of us win. The Bible tells me not to covet my neighbor's wife or his servants or his animals or anything about my neighbor (Exodus 20:17). That includes his marriage. Taking time to check out someone else's marriage only detracts from giving mine all I have.

Marriage-help

To see if your marriage might be suffering from marriage-envy or hopes for perfection, check the following. Over the past year, how many of these have you done?

Circle one:

1. Read a book about marriage: 1 2 3 4 more
2. Attended seminars
    on marriage: 1 2 3 4 more
3. Listened to tapes on marriage: 1 2 3 4 more
4. Attended church meetings
    on marriage: 1 2 3 4 more
5. Taken classes on related subjects
    (personal communication,
    relationships, etc.):   1 2 3 4 more

Each of these can be healthy in proper dosages, but make sure you aren't on a marriage-help binge. If our marriages need this much help, maybe we need to go to a counselor and get direct assistance. Don't let marriage-help kill your marriage.

Creative Approach

A creative couple will take some guidance and add to it their own innovative approach to marriage. They set their own goals, both immediate and long-range, and make plans as to how to reach those ends. Always willing to learn from others, they do not care to act out a role written by someone else — no matter how clever that part.

I've counseled couples who have rattled off a litany of authors, radio personalities, ministers and movie stars. They have chanted, "Dr. Mucksmuck says couples should brush their teeth together." Or, "Rev. Know-So says husbands should take the lead in prayer." Or, "Counselor Who says I need to manage the money."

Unable or unwilling to control their own lives, many couples are afraid to make a move without getting some authority to confirm it. They need to take their marriage out from under the microscope and let it live.

Be free to make your own mistakes. Have the dignity to make your own choices. Know the pleasure of claiming your own victories.

Counselors, ministers, books and seminars are all good avenues. But don't work your marriage to death.

Centering on Strengths

When you do look for help, lean more toward people and literature which major on strengths. Programs and philosophies which center on handling problems may create more problems. Some couples see marriage as a necessary evil, fraught with danger and flooded in despair. When we major in difficulties we are prone to see more of them than actually exist.

It's not unlike yawning. If we sit around and talk about it long enough, soon everyone in the room will be stretching, bleary-eyed and open-jowled. Marriage seems to create problems when we concentrate on those blips.

The Bible tells us:

Finally, brothers, whatever is true, whatever is noble, whatever is right, whatever is pure, whatever is lovely, whatever is admirable—if anything is excellent or praiseworthy—think about such things (Philippians 4:8).

An elderly lady had a pain in her shoulder. The doctor prescribed medication for her and after several weeks the pain was gone. Hardly a month went by before she was back with a pain in her knee and the doctor started all over again.

Soon it became apparent that the lady was pain-centered. She needed a pain and the attention it brought. She saw herself as a person with problems and she liked to focus on them.

Similarly, some couples move from agony to agony. They could shift to living from celebration to celebration but they aren't used to that kind of focus. It's as if they have a vacuum which can be filled only with disappointment.

That attitude will wear a marriage.

Move from joy to joy. Focus on the great happinesses of marriage.

Flexercise

1. What are a few of the strengths in your marriage?

2. How is you marriage better this year than it was last year?

3. What happy dream would you like to fulfill next year?

*E*mergency *R*elief

IF YOUR MARRIAGE has reached a critical point and something must be done immediately, consider the following steps you might take.

Instant Action

Back off.

Lower the heat for a few minutes, maybe a few hours. A walk around the block probably will help.

Control your voice.

Try to get hold of yourself rationally. Act, sound and look like a reasonable person. Breathe deeply several times.

Talk to yourself.

Tell yourself everything will work out. You must convince yourself before you try to calm your mate.

Apologize.

Without reservation, without extra clauses, without blaming your spouse, simply and directly say you are sorry and take time to say specifically what you are sorry about. Blanket apologies accomplish little.

Explain you will return.

Five minutes, fifty minutes, two hours, whatever. If you are going to back off, tell your partner when you will return. He needs to know you are dropping out for short relief and plan to bounce back. That message provides space, hope and security, all at the same time.

Check Vital Signs

Articulate the problem.

Make sure that both of you understand the problem. Don't assume. Don't guess. Give your spouse ample time to explain the situation in detail. Don't rush him. Don't talk over him.

Reword the problem.

Describe the problem in your own words so your partner will know you understand. Don't argue or change part of the problem. Your job now is to make sure you are both dealing with the same issue.

Ask questions.

If there is any part of the situation that you don't understand, ask for a further explanation. Do not correct or accuse or counterattack.

Assure your willingness.

Let your partner know you want to work on this. Don't bluff. You don't need a solution now but you must express a sincere willingness to work on it. Few things will hurt a relationship as badly as broken promises. Read that sentence out loud.

Ask for suggestions.

What would your partner like to see change immediately? If possible, promise to look into it. You understand this brings pain to your spouse and you would like to correct the problem. You are on the right road now.

Intermediate Relief

Change locations.

Friday night you will go out for coffee. You will take paper and pencil and work on a solution. A change of location is often refreshing, creative and loving, and it promises undivided attention.

Suggest alterations.

What can be changed over the next week or two that could help? Come home earlier? Come to bed earlier? Go out on a date? Buy a new dress?

No long-term changes at this point. Don't sell the car, the house or the children.

Relief can come now through small changes. The big things might take a few more weeks.

Get some input.

Ask if you need insights into your marriage. Do you need to read a book, take a class, visit with a friend, see a counselor? Do whatever is helpful and mutually beneficial. Don't be proud. Information, experience and wisdom could energize most of us.

Take a trip.

If boredom and burnout from routine are at the root of your friction, a weekend away is likely to give you room to exercise your love. When you come back, you may have a desire to conquer most of life's struggles.

Long-Range Relief

Find new places for communication.

If a meal at a restaurant once a week is not practical, go for a coffee break. All of us need a time and a place where our accounts can be kept current. Ask for a booth.

These do not have to be horrendous, nerve-racking sessions. They can be uplifting looks at the future.

Find new forms of communication.

Promise direct communication with light humor.

Look for new hobbies and interests.

Agree to find two things this year that you can do together. Hiking, bowling, golf, charities, church work, skiing, cards, Bible study. Two things that will not create competition between you but will develop partnerships and satisfaction.

Consider new jobs and cities.

If serious moves are warranted, don't be afraid to make them. Be sure the decisions are not made harshly or without forethought. If you merely intend to take the same problems to a new city, not much will be accomplished.

Make this promise. Your relationship is more important than any career consideration, and you will keep it that way. That's hard for many of us to accomplish in a consumer society, but by now you probably are willing to be that committed.

Taking a Pledge

When the fur begins to fly, we have trouble keeping a cool head. While you are calm, sane, and madly in love, each of you take the pledges on the following page.

**WHEN OUR RELATIONSHIP GETS HOT AND HARRIED,
I PROMISE I WILL:**

Never hit

Never call your mother names

Never use our dating days as ammunition

Never call you names

Never threaten to get even

Never compare us with friends

Never yell (very loud)

Never say, "I told you so"

Never throw anything

Never pout, cry or sulk (for long)

Never slam more than two doors

Never use any words you have to look up

Never say always or never

Never put mean things in writing (only kind comments)

Never change the setting on your alarm

In response, you each pledge to do the following:

**IN ADDITION, AND BECAUSE I LOVE YOU,
I PROMISE I WILL:**

Always be quick to forgive

Always calm down before bedtime

Always apologize

Always fix breakfast the next day

Always accept *slightly* more blame than I deserve

Always say, "I love you."

NOTE: If you have made it all the way through the pledges above, I commend you — and you don't need a **Flexercise** to put this chapter to work.

*B*laming *O*thers

ONE OF THE SURE SIGNS of burnout is when we get heavily into the blame business. We have, in effect, stopped taking life as it comes and have dropped out to find fault. This is an indication that we have become weary and disillusioned. We have lost our emotional energy and our marriage has fallen into dangerous doldrums.

Suppose a husband and wife have stopped dating. They never go out for an evening and have settled for long evenings watching re-runs of *Gilligan's Island.*

She tells herself, *I know why we don't go out anymore. It's because his mother always wants to go.*

He says to himself, *We don't go out because she always complains about how much we spend.*

The couple does not discuss their impasse. They make no attempt to hurdle the wall; they simply dig in and blame each other.

But we've tried this before, he reasons. *We go out a few times and she starts to squawk. I don't need it.*

She mumbles to herself, *The minute we mention going out I can hear his mother shuffling along. I'd rather eat in the basement.*

High-Centered

As long as they concentrate on blame, they will remain high-centered. The snow is holding their wheels off the ground and they cannot move forward. Fruitlessly the wheels spin furiously in midair.

Blame is a severe subject. Couples are often in the blame business for decades. She knows it's his fault she got pregnant. He blames her for the fact that he never went to college. They blame each other for their lack of friends. They are stuck because they cannot move away from accusations.

We have been taught and trained to blame others for what goes on. Supposedly our mothers are the reasons we never became astronauts. It's our teachers' fault we never became corporation moguls. Our brothers stood in the way of our becoming fashion models. The list goes on endlessly. By buying into this approach we absolve ourselves of any need to try. Someone else has reportedly sealed our fate. It's an ugly, debilitating business. The underlying message is that there is no reason to try.

Justice vs. Mercy

The need to identify the crime, capture the culprit and extract a confession may be too strong. It also may be too self-serving.

Often we hide behind the Sherlock Holmes Syndrome. We act as though perfect justice must be served or our dignity will never be appeased. Poor us.

While it is true that some injustices must be addressed, others are better ignored. If we go through life demanding redress, reparations and equality, we are going to have a collection of bruises that would make any abstractionist painter drool with envy.

Justice belongs in courtrooms—the places Jesus told us to avoid. Marriages are better served by the sound attributes of mercy, grace and forgiveness. These allow us to overlook certain blemishes:

- They help us forget insults.
- They permit us to forgo reparations.

- They prohibit revenge.

- They short-cut the long accusatory process.

- They limit the time we feel sorry for ourselves.

Casting blame struggles with evil. Mercy, grace and forgiveness touch hands with the divine: "God . . . is rich in mercy" (Ephesians 2:4).

Love reaches its hand across the table and says, "I'm sorry we feel far apart. Let's jump in the car and go get ice cream." Justice is still arguing over who bought the ice cream last time.

The Purpose of Blame

If you are caught on the treadmill of blame, you are serving some inner purpose. We can walk off a treadmill any time we choose. It is not a cage. We are not shackled hand or foot. Look at the following list and see if one or more of these keeps you from setting yourself free:

- Blaming others helps us avoid making decisions.

- Blaming others helps us feel sorry for ourselves.

- Blaming others helps us distance ourselves from
  our mates.

- Blaming others helps us hold off being kind.

- Blaming others helps us manipulate others.

- Blaming others helps us take the spotlight off our
  mistakes.

- Blaming others helps us hide behind our own in-
  securities.

- Blaming others helps us hold back mercy, grace
  and forgiveness.

Maybe this list does not fit your purpose exactly, but

it must suggest some clues. Our motives are frequently hidden in the overstuffed couches of our hearts. You might want to dig a bit deeper for yourself.

Whatever need it serves, we can believe there is a reason we do not do something to create a better situation. Blame is working for us. It has become a friend. We are reluctant to lay it down until we have a satisfactory device to take its place.

Ready Reconciliation

Why do we often trust blame more than we do reconciliation? Why are we more at home with war than we are with peace?

These questions lead to more questions, but some answers are possible. Were we accustomed to war in our youth? Do we have war in our job? Do we wage war in our heart? Do we live a continuous battle and carry it over into our home? Have we developed a war mentality which makes us uncomfortable with peace? Certainly some of us have.

To live with accusation is to drive with our brakes on — we are burning rubber simply because we don't release those brakes.

One couple comes to mind who seemingly came into marriage with a combat mentality. Their approach to relationship was one of suspicion and distrust.

"I don't worry about Mike running around." Betty's forehead was rigid. "He won't get out of my sight. He knows he has to be home evenings and I'll see to it he is."

Betty came from a family where her father was terribly undependable and she watched her mother fight for her "rights." The idea of a trusting relationship was in fact foreign to Betty. She could count on what she could control and nothing else.

It won't be easy for Betty to learn the values of reconciliation. She is more content to stand at arm's length and protect herself. With time and work she may some day be able to live at peace with Mike, but Mike will have to learn to live at peace also.

Couples who maintain an amount of distrust for each other which is comfortable to them are heavy into external security systems. Couples who simply fall into each other's arms with total trust have their own built-in security system.

Our Experience With God

It may be easier to understand if we think about our relationship with God. Before Jesus Christ came into our lives there was a wall between us and God. We weren't comfortable with each other because of this barrier.

When we asked Christ into our heart, God tore the wall down. Today we have ready access to each other; we have a high degree of trust, acceptance and love. We are reconciled to God because of what Christ did for us on the cross (2 Corinthians 5:18,19).

Married couples can draw on that experience and tear down the walls between themselves. Every wall, partition, divider, curtain or shade we remove from our relationship just brings us that much closer to each other. The closer we become, the less blame and distrust we will hold.

Our marriage experience and our redemption experience are not the same; however, our redemption does give us a loving example to draw upon.

Crippling Self-Blame

Frequently we meet a husband (or wife) who burns up his marriage with self-blame. He knows everything is his fault; in his eyes he messes everything up; he is pretty well disgusted with himself.

That in itself is bad enough, but he allows the self-blame to render him inoperative. He doesn't want to go anywhere, do anything or take any risks because he knows he will mess up.

Blame by itself is too useless to entertain. Nothing good comes from it. If we are caught in the tentacles of guilt feelings, we owe it to ourselves and our marriage to find help. Discuss your feelings with a spiritual leader and let him help you break free.

If I can point my finger at what I did wrong, name the bugger and correct the situation, I have behaved responsibly. But to let phantom guilt run around the halls of my marriage serves no good purpose.

Marriage on the move is unlikely to burn out. Marriage that stops to pick up accusations or to sulk or pout adds a terrible load to the vehicle.

Flexercise

---

1. Have you ever stayed home because the two of you were blaming each other? Explain.

2. Which of you is more insistent that you agree on whose fault it was?

3. When did you last tell your spouse it was your fault? When did he last say it was his fault?

Every Partner Needs a Manual

PICTURE IT. A couple is standing at the altar exchanging vows, promising to do all the appropriate things. When they finish, the minister doesn't ask them to produce their wedding rings. Instead he asks for the manuals. In solemn reverence the bride and groom hand each other a colorful manual, pages bound with a huge, white satin shoestring.

This unorthodox manual contains instructions on how the bride or groom operate. Each page has an appropriate title including:

Temperament	High Points
Feeding Instructions	Low Points
Emergency Procedures	Checkups
Hang-ups	Beliefs
Fears	Misconceptions
Sensitivities	Prejudices
Ideas of Fun	Sense of Humor

Every appliance in our house has an operator's manual, or a maintenance manual, or some set of directions. It would seem only reasonable for marriage partners each to have instructions on the upkeep, parts, replacement and oiling of the other.

Preparing a Manual on Our Spouse

Since his (or her) mother is unlikely to provide us with a suitable booklet, we will have to construct our own. We will consciously study our partner and learn what makes her tick. We will suffer fewer breakdowns and less malfunctioning if we understand how his machine works. We will experience less friction, less rub, less drag, less downtime and less burnout because we practice preventive maintenance and give our partner regular checkups.

Wishing he were like someone else wastes precious minutes. Spend your time playing to his strengths. That's true for both husbands and wives.

Ask certain key questions about your partner:

- When are her down hours during the day?
- What kind of food does he particularly like?
- What subjects is she sensitive about?
- What weekend activity will put him in high gear?
- How can I feed my partner's self-esteem?
- How does he really feel about criticism?
- What frightens her?

The list goes on. Maybe you'd like to add some questions that are important to you.

If necessary, write the answer down, identifying your spouse's characteristics. If possible, share your observations with your spouse. For example, tell him, "I realize that right after work is a bad time for us to discuss our family problems. Let's agree to wait until after we have finished eating and the dishes are done."

Brad explained, "I learned not to hit Sherri with everything when she first arrives home. I get home first and am high on energy when she comes in the door. But dumping everything I know on her at that moment seems to drown her. After four years of marriage I've finally learned to turn my burners down until Sherri has been home for an hour or so."

Studying our mate is not devious. Mapping out our partner's terrain is not surreptitious. Playing up to our spouse's strengths and weaknesses is not a subservient role. These are honorable moves practiced by loving and devoted husbands and wives.

Stubborn Resistance

Too many marriage partners appear to study their mates for the purpose of aggravating them. They know what will anger their spouses so they make sure to do it. This is sadistic.

"It always irked Hank when supper was ten minutes late," said Sally, "so I would sometimes stretch it out to fifteen minutes, maybe twenty. Just long enough to get him red around the ears. He shouldn't get so upset about things like that, so I needed to teach him a lesson."

I never met Hank but I assume he wasn't a mule. One can only wonder how much more she might have taught him with kindness and reason.

Some of us consider needling an effective tool to bring about change. In reality needling punctures, creates pain, and brings on resentment. Creative partners find caring, positive ways to improve the people they love.

Sandy provokes her husband Dave simply to get attention. She knows how to set him off and does it periodically because she can't stand being ignored. Dave keeps his tools in methodical order. Sandy will hide a screwdriver or a hammer just to hear him blow steam. She has studied him well and uses that information to provoke him.

Dave and Sandy are an interesting couple. They have failed to learn constructive forms of communication so they resort to what they do know—agitation. It must work in a way because they have stayed together for decades. Unfortunately, their relationship has been a volatile, high risk and often painful one.

If an evening is too quiet, Dave will say, "Have you heard from your brother? I bet he still hasn't found a job." Dave isn't stupid. He knows that will cure an otherwise boring evening.

Sensitivity Level

No one need apologize for being sensitive to his partner's needs. This is not a servant's role but a lover's. Sharp people know when to confront, when to support and when to back off and let the other person fly alone.

Being sensitive and babying a partner are not the same. "Babying" a person is to continuously coddle, give in and let him run the show. Sensitivity says, "We all have high and low points—strengths and weaknesses. I have enough sense to allow you room for those dimensions. Hopefully you will be able to reciprocate."

Why do we need to study our partner? Shouldn't sensitivity come naturally? No, it shouldn't come easily. People are different. That's what makes us individuals. When we declare that we understand people, we miss the point. The person we are married to is a fascinating creation of God, complete with diamonds, gold, stone and rust. Part of life's greatest adventure is to get to know that unique person. The psalmist says he will meditate on God's "wonderful works" (145:5). Our spouse is one of those marvels.

A Success Story

Jan was a city girl who gave her love to a country boy. She left her paved streets, corner drugstore and well-manicured neighborhood to live in Bob's open fields and quiet dirt roads.

At first it was hard, harder than she had expected. Jan missed many of the sights and sounds. A couple of times she felt sorry for herself. Some of her closest friends were a hound dog and a troublesome crow. Jan drove more trucks than she did cars.

Slowly and steadily Jan turned her new setting into a laboratory. She began to study her new environment and started to map out her husband. She found the highs and the lows. She looked for the hope they could share.

Soon Jan found herself blending into her mate, and in response his lifestyle moved toward hers.

Twenty-five years later you meet a lady who has loved her life, her children and her man. Jan mapped out a way to know her man and she became one with his life.

Every married person needs to study his spouse and work at fitting together—both males and females.

Flexercise

---

1. Where would your mate most like to go to eat?

2. What could you do at home that would most likely make your spouse's life go easier?

3. If you wanted to go on vacation, what would be the best way to approach the subject with your partner?

The Spirit of Love

D AN AND BEVERLY WERE the kind of couple you would expect to see smiling on a box of breakfast cereal. Freckle-faced and rosy-cheeked, they chiseled out a living in the sandhills of western Nebraska. They dressed casually in boots, jeans and cowboy shirts.

Their three children finished off a package that had "All-American Family" written all across the front. You knew they were good people.

Only when you talked to Dan and Bev alone did you sense that things weren't right. He clammed up and she fidgeted, never looking in his direction. Steam had built up but was locked inside each of them, and it was simply a matter of time before the lid would blow.

I had known them for just a few days at a retreat when Dan pulled me aside. His face was relieved and relaxed.

"I know what the problem was," Dan said abruptly. "I never understood what the tension was until now. Back when Beverly and I were going together, she had a date with another guy. All these years I've been angry over that.

"We never talked about it, but it has been a source of pain for us all these years. Tonight, for the first time I can say I have forgiven her."

Dan had taken one problem, one "failure," one oversight, and made it last for ten years. Neither Dan nor Bev could be free of the pain as long as he refused to forgive her.

Forgiveness Applied

Any couple who lives together will have to apply forgiveness in liberal doses. If we think that withholding our forgiveness and love is a good teaching tool, we create unnecessary and agonizing pressure on the very relationship we have sworn to protect.

It sounded so final when Marge said, "I will never be able to love Jay again. His affair has driven all caring from my heart."

"I don't love him anymore" sounds concrete, immovable and hopeless. But in Marge's case it wasn't. She decided to allow the Holy Spirit to fill her heart with new love for Jay. Marge asked God to supply her with His love and she directed it toward her husband. What might normally have crumbled was re-established as she gained more love than she thought possible.

Romans 5:5 spells out both the principle and the promise: "And hope does not disappoint us, because God has poured out his love into our hearts by the Holy Spirit, whom he has given us."

When we became Christians, God flooded us with His love by means of the Holy Spirit. This love resides in us because of our relationship with God. The question is whether or not we choose to tap that love and apply it to our marriage.

The evidence is substantial that many couples are allowing this love to overflow toward each other. Not only do we have the testimonies of spouses who use it, but we also have statistics which support it. Survey after survey, conducted by universities and other institutions, reveal that a high degree of "strong" or "successful" marriages attribute their unity to a healthy faith in God. These couples believe God supplies them with additional love.

A number of marriages have a constant tension because of a love/hate relationship. They have many reasons to be ecstatic with each other, but at the same time they have collected hundreds of little nicks, scars, insults, broken promises and dents. As we gather and store these bad experiences, we become loaded down with regrets and unsettled scores. If we never discard this load of "junk," our marriage becomes too heavy to carry.

Fortunately the Holy Spirit supplies enough love to clean up the trash that has accumulated in our relationships. Love allows me to toss out the garbage and never miss it.

Agape Love

A biblical concept of love is broad enough to cover every situation. Couples are taught to use both *eros* love and *agape* love. *Eros* love is based on attractiveness. We want to love someone because he is appealing. He looks good, has a twinkle in his eye and actually feels good. Related to sex appeal, this is a valid form of love. While it can be risky, God created us with a sense of *eros* and we need not apologize for fulfilling its desire in a married context. On the contrary we probably should avoid marrying someone for whom we have no sensual draw. In short, our partner should give us some form of the hots.

The Song of Solomon is a terrific illustration of *eros* love at its best. When Jacob saw Rachel (Genesis 29:18) he went bonkers at the sensual reality.

But what happens on the days when the spouse doesn't look so swift? What about the times when his attitude is dismal? How do we react when she tells us to buzz off?

That is when we put God's *agape* love to work. This is the love God has for us despite our inconsistencies, failures and sin. He continues to *agape*—love us and He enables us to love our partner when she is lower than mud.

"The fruit of the Spirit is love *[agape]*" (Galatians 5:22), love that is not dependent on the loveliness of the person but on the intention of the lover. The Holy Spirit supplies that type of love to the person who is filled with the Spirit.

Every couple can be strengthened by both types of love: *eros* and *agape*. We don't become pseudo-spiritual and ignore *eros*. Neither do we dare base our marriage solely on *agape* and exclude *eros* love.

There is a nauseating commercial on television in which the wife is looking forward to going out dancing. After some discussion about the product, her husband asks what she would say if they simply stayed home instead of dancing. She replies that she would say, "See your lawyer."

Most marriages are not that superficial, but some are. *Agape* love is the Spirit-filled ability to love in both the rough and the pleasant times.

Love Applied

Does that sound like a bunch of hocus-pocus? Should we expect a magic wand to sweep across our relationship and turn us into love doves? Not exactly, but let's spell out precisely how it works.

1. We ask God.

We want His Spirit to flood our life with love. That is tapping the resource. God helps make us more caring, sensitive, thoughtful and patient, all of the first-class ingredients that create a loving person (Galatians 5:22).

2. Ask for instruction.

The Bible is packed with teaching (1 Corinthians 13) and excellent examples of relational love (Song of Solomon, etc.). We want to know more of what love is and how to use it.

3. Center on a person.

In this case the focal point is our marriage partner. We ask for guidance on how we can demonstrate compassion, friendship, helpfulness, fidelity, cheerfulness and other attributes toward the person we have married.

To be filled with the Spirit is to be filled with Jesus Christ. His control means He also controls our love.

Even if a couple says, "We don't love each other anymore," the situation is far from hopeless. We do control love and its flow. That is the added strength of the Christian life. It is possible for love to rise up from the ashes and to show tremendous energy and vitality.

The Marriage Dip

Practically every relationship will drop down into the dumps at one time or another. The dip may last a week or two; it could carry on for a year.

Those who have a firm handle on love are likely to face fewer dips, and the dips they do face tend to be of shorter duration. They find love as a renewable resource. If love is "called up" from God and applied with expectation, they feel confident that love will reign again in their relationship.

Any couple with this practical anticipation can find a way to recover from the potholes of marriage. As the author of Hebrews wrote: "We are confident of better things" (6:9).

"We had a number of tough years," Bob admitted, shaking his head. "We were broke; had kids running all over the place; my job was driving me crazy. But our love seemed to hold through it all.

"There was a spirituality that kept taking us back to Christ and what He was doing in our lives. It's so much easier now, but even in those early days, though our love stretched and strained, it held."

Living Marriages

Whenever a marriage takes a dip, whether simple or severe, the message is the same: Marriage can live again. Most couples who are determined to spend themselves for the relationship have a high probability of maintaining stability. Many marriages that are not working—could.

If an average couple can survive hard times and prosper through hard work, they are even more likely to survive with spiritual strength. Our connection in Jesus Christ supplies the resources so vital to a lasting relationship. Tolerance, forgiveness, empathy and thoughtfulness are all virtues which are energized by Christ.

Currently marriage is getting some bad press and much of it is warranted. There is something wrong with our society and with our hearts, but there is nothing wrong with the concept of marriage. When God created the idea of two people committed to each other for life, He knew exactly how good that could be. We as humans agree on how fulfilling a marriage relationship should be. There isn't anything wrong with the plan.

With some help we can learn how to keep the fuel supply high in our relationship. By doing that on a regular basis we can avert the burnout and thank God sincerely for the person we have married.

Flexercise

1. How does your closeness to Christ increase your capacity to love?

2. Have you ever felt a serious "dip" in your marriage? How did you pull out of it?

3. What are some of the good reasons God gave us marriage?

Conclusion

The Happy Prospect

After 27 years I would not trade marriage for any other lifestyle. It continues to be fulfilling, enriching, great fun — and a pain in the neck. Small price to pay, though, for this much reward.

Pat and I are still plotting, planning and conniving ways to make it a better marriage. We thank God for the hope and satisfaction each year brings.

We are encouraged because of the thousands of happy marriages we see. The twinkle is still in these couples' eyes, the excitement still in their voices, and commitment serves as their anchor.

Couples and families are not only making it but doing it well. Hold each other every day and praise God for the joy you have together. He has given you one of life's greatest gifts.